8086/88 Assembly Language Programming

Leo J. Scanlon

BRADY COMMUNICATIONS COMPANY, INC.
A Prentice-Hall Publishing Company
Bowie, MD

8086/88 Assembly Language Programming

Library of Congress Cataloging in Publication Data

Scanlon, Leo J.
    8086/88 assembly language programming.

    Includes index.
    1. Intel 8086 (Microprocessor)—Programming.   2. Intel 8088 (Microprocessor)—Programming.   3. Assembler language (Computer program language)   I. Title.
    QA76.8.I292S29 1984   001.64'2   84–251

ISBN 0-89303-424-X

Prentice-Hall International, Inc., London
Prentice-Hall Canada, Inc., Scarborough, Ontario
Prentice-Hall of Australia, Pty., Ltd., Sydney
Prentice-Hall of India Private Limited, New Delhi
Prentice-Hall of Japan, Inc., Tokyo
Prentice-Hall of Southeast Asia Pte. Ltd., Singapore
Whitehall Books, Limited, Petone, New Zealand
Editora Prentice-Hall Do Brasil LTDA., Rio de Janeiro

Printed in the United States of America

    85 86 87 88 89 90 91 92 93 94   10 9 8 7 6 5 4 3

Publishing Director: David Culverwell
Acquisitions Editor: Terrell Anderson
Text Designer/Production Editor: Michael J. Rogers
Manufacturing Director: John Komsa
Art Director/Cover Design: Don Sellers
Assistant Art Director: Bernard Vervin

Copy Editor: Keith R. Tidman
Typesetter: Electronic Publishing Services, Baltimore, MD
Printer: R. R. Donnelley & Sons Company, Harrisonburg, VA
Typefaces: Helvetica (display), Palatino (text), and Universal monotype #3 H-P (computer programs)

The photos of the 8086 and 8088 microprocessors are courtesy of Intel Corporation.

Trademarks of Material Mentioned in This Text

Limits of Liability and Disclaimer of Warranty

Contents

Preface

Why Assembly Language?

Many people write all of their computer programs in one of the so-called "high-level languages," particularly BASIC. BASIC is easy to learn, easy to use, and fast enough for most computing tasks. That being the case, why would anyone want to use any other language? One reason is that BASIC, like human languages, is not well-suited to everything. Some tasks are much easier in other languages. Imagine, for example, trying to describe fine cooking without some French words or symphonies without some Italian words. Similarly, special computing tasks like graphics, music, or word processing are often easier in special languages.

Furthermore, BASIC is quite slow. The term "slow" may surprise the beginner, since short programs seem to run instantaneously. Problems do occur, however, in the following situations:

1. When large amounts of data are involved. You will notice how slow BASIC is when a program must, for example, sort a long list of names and addresses or accounts. Similarly, BASIC will be quite slow when a program must search though a 50-page report or keep inventory records on thousands of items.

2. When graphics are involved. If a program is drawing a picture on the screen, it must work quickly or the delay will be intolerable. If objects in the picture are supposed to move, the program must be fast enough to make the motion look natural. This is particularly difficult when the picture contains many objects (such as space ships, base stations, and alien invaders), all of which are moving in different directions.

3. When a lot of decisions or "thinking" is required. This is often necessary in complex games like checkers or chess. The program has to try many possibilities and decide on a reasonable move. Obviously, the more possibilities there are and the more analysis is required, the longer it will take the computer to move.

Why is BASIC slow? In the first place, the computer actually translates each BASIC statement into simple internal commands (so-called machine or assembly language). It does this every time it runs the BASIC program. Thus, much of the computer's time is spent translating the program, not running it.

There are versions of BASIC called *compilers* that perform the translation once and then save the translated version. BASIC would still be slow, however, because of its mechanical nature. It is really like an automobile with an automatic transmission; no amount of coaxing can ever get you the performance or fuel economy that a skillful driver can achieve with a manual transmission. The human being is simply a more flexible, more skillful, and smarter operator than is the automatic transmission or the BASIC interpreter or compiler.

Assembly language is the computer equivalent of a manual transmission. It gives the programmer greater control over the computer at the cost of more work, more detail, and less convenience. Like an automatic transmission, BASIC is good enough most of the time for most programmers. But for those who must get maximum performance from their computers, assembly language is essential. You will find that most complex games, graphics programs, and large business programs are written at least partially in assembly language.

Even if assembly language *is* your likely choice, you may be wondering whether you have enough background to learn assembly language programming. You *do* if you have done some programming of *any* kind. If you know BASIC or some other high-level language, that's fine. If you have developed programs in an assembly language, that's even better. For the benefit of former high-level language users, the book has two starting points.

If you have never programmed in assembly language, start with Chapter 0, which gives you a "crash course" in the *binary* and *hexadecimal* numbering systems. Otherwise, if you already know what these terms mean and understand how to use them, proceed directly to Chapter 1.

The Contents of This Book

In Chapter 1, we introduce 8086 and 8088 microprocessors—the computer's "brain"— and discuss the differences between them.

Chapter 2 discusses assemblers in general, then describes the Intel ASM–86 assembler. Every assembler that runs on an 8086- or 8088-based computer has most or all of the features of ASM–86.

Chapter 3 describes the instruction set that the 8086 and 8088 share. These are the commands you use to communicate with your computer. *This book treats the instructions in functional groups, rather than alphabetically.* That is, we group add with subtract, multiply with divide, and so on. Through this approach you not only get to *understand* what the instructions do, but you also appreciate how they fit together.

Chapter 4 tells you how to combine instructions to perform extended math operations that the microprocessor's instruction set doesn't provide directly. Chapter 5 covers operations on lists and tables.

In Chapter 6, you learn how to convert keyboard data to numbers the computer can process. You also learn how to convert numbers to a form in which the screen can display them. Finally, in Chapter 7, we discuss the 8087 Numeric Data Processor, a chip that performs mathematical calculations.

The book provides four appendices for your convenience. Appendix A has tables that help you convert hexadecimal numbers to decimal, or vice versa. Appendix B summarizes the ASCII character set. Appendices C and D summarize the 8086/8088 instruction set in alphabetical order, and show how long it takes to execute each instruction, how many bytes each instruction occupies in memory, and which status flags it affects.

Study Exercises

Most chapters conclude with a set of questions and programming exercises. Some of these test your understanding of the material in the chapter, whereas others are meant to extend your knowledge of the material into additional, related topics.

Supplementary Reference Books

This book contains the details most people need to know about the ASM–86 assembly language. For more information, get a copy of Intel's *An Introduction to ASM–86*.

Further, if you are designing add-on hardware for the computer, or just want to have the full details on the chips in the system, you may want to get one or more of the following reference documents:

- *iAPX 86,88 User's Manual* and Numeric Supplement
- *iAPX 86/10 Data Sheet*
- *iAPX 88/10 Data Sheet*

To order, contact Intel Corporation, Literature Dept., 3065 Bowers Ave., Santa Clara, CA 95051.

May you have as much satisfaction developing assembly lanuage programs as I had writing this book.

Leo J. Scanlon

0

A Crash Course in Computer Numbering Systems

Unless you are visiting from another planet, you have spent your entire life counting things using decimal numbers. Decimal is the *base 10* numbering system, which means it has 10 digits, 0 through 9.

Human beings are quite comfortable counting in decimal (probably because we have ten fingers and ten toes), but computers are not. Instead, they count with the base 2 (or *binary*) numbering system, which has only two digits, 0 and 1. Hence, to communicate with the computer at its own level (as you do when you program in assembly language), you must be familiar with binary numbering. In addition to binary, assembly language programmers also use another numbering system— base 16 (or *hexadecimal*)—so you must be familiar with it as well.

This chapter is a ''crash course'' in computer numbering systems for readers who have no previous exposure to them. That's why we call it Chapter 0. If you already understand binary and hexadecimal numbering, feel free to skip this chapter and begin at Chapter 1.

0.1 The Binary Numbering System

A computer gets all program instructions and data from its *memory*. Memory is comprised of integrated circuits (or ''chips'') that contain thousands of electrical components. These components act like light switches in that they have only two possible settings: ''On'' or ''Off.''

Still, with only these two settings, combinations of memory components can represent numbers of any size. How? Read on.

The On and Off settings of a memory component correspond to the two digits of the *binary numbering system*, the fundamental system for computers. Having only two digits, 1 (On) and 0 (Off), the binary numbering system is a *base 2* system. Again, this contrasts with the standard decimal numbering system, which has 10 digits (0 through 9).

The switch-like components of memory are called "bits," short for *binary digits*. By convention, a bit that is On has the value 1 and a bit that is Off has the value 0. This appears to be woefully limiting, until you consider that a decimal digit (no, it's not called a "det") can range only from 0 to 9. Just as you can combine decimal digits to form numbers larger than 9, you can combine binary digits to form numbers larger than 1.

As you know, to represent a decimal number larger than 9 requires another digit, a "tens position" digit. Likewise, to represent a decimal number larger than 99 requires a "hundreds position" digit, and so on. Each decimal digit you add has a *weight* of 10 times the digit to its immediate right.

For example, you can represent the decimal number 324 as

$$(3 \times 100) + (2 \times 10) + (4 \times 1)$$

or as

$$(3 \times 10^2) + (2 \times 10^1) + (4 \times 10^0)$$

So, in more mathematical terms, each decimal digit is a power of 10 greater than the preceding digit.

A similar rule applies to the binary numbering system. In this system, *each binary digit is a power of two greater than the preceding digit*. The right-most bit has a weight of 2^0 (decimal 1), the next bit has a weight of 2^1 (decimal 2), and so on. For example, the binary number 101 has a decimal value of five, because

$$
\begin{aligned}
101_2 &= (1 \times 2^2) + (0 \times 2^1) + (1 \times 2^0) \\
&= (1 \times 4) + (0 \times 2) + (1 \times 1) \\
&= 5_{10}
\end{aligned}
$$

Do you now understand how binary numbers are constructed? To find the value of any given bit position, you double the weight of the preceding bit position. Thus, the binary weights of the first eight bits are 1, 2, 4, 8, 16, 32, 64, and 128. Figure 0–1 summarizes these weights.

To convert a decimal value to binary, you make a series of simple subtractions. Each subtraction gives you the value of a single binary digit (bit).

To begin, subtract the largest possible binary weight from the decimal value and enter a 1 in that bit position. Then subtract the next largest

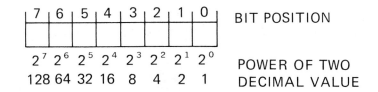

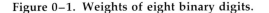

Figure 0–1. Weights of eight binary digits.

possible binary weight from the result and enter a 1 in *that* bit position. Continue until the result is zero. Enter a 0 in any bit position whose weight cannot be subtracted from the current decimal value. For example, to convert decimal 50 to binary:

$$
\begin{array}{r}
50 \\
-32 \\
\hline
18 \\
-16 \\
\hline
2 \\
-\ 2 \\
\hline
0
\end{array}
\quad
\begin{array}{l}
\\
\text{Bit position } 5 = 1 \\
\\
\text{Bit position } 4 = 1 \\
\\
\text{Bit position } 1 = 1
\end{array}
$$

Entering a 0 in the other bit positions (Bits 3, 2, and 0) yields a final result of 110010.

To verify that the binary equivalent of decimal 50 is indeed 110010, add the decimal weights of the "1" positions:

$$
\begin{array}{rl}
32 & \text{(Bit 5)} \\
16 & \text{(Bit 4)} \\
+\ 2 & \text{(Bit 1)} \\
\hline
50 &
\end{array}
$$

Eight Bits Make a Byte

The Apple II and III, Commodore 64 and VIC-20, Radio Shack TRS-80, and many other popular microcomputers are designed around an 8-bit *microprocessor*. Eight-bit microprocessors are so named because they process information 8 bits at a time. To process more than 8 bits, they must perform additional operations.

In computer jargon, an 8-bit unit of information is called a *byte*. With 8 bits, a byte can represent decimal values from 0 (binary 00000000) to 255 (binary 11111111).

Because a byte is the fundamental unit of processing, microcomputers are described in terms of the number of bytes (rather than bits) their memories can hold. Further, microcomputer manufacturers generally construct memory in blocks of 1,024 bytes. This particular quantity reflects the binary orientation of computers in that it represents 2^{10} bytes.

The value 1,024 has a standard abbreviation, the letter *K*. Hence, an advertisement for a computer that has a "48K memory" tells you that the computer has 48 × 1,024 (or 49,152) bytes of memory.

Adding Binary Numbers

You add binary numbers the same way you add decimal numbers: by carrying any excess from one column to the next. For example, if you add the decimal values 7 and 9, you must carry a 1 into the "tens" column to produce the correct result (16). Similarly, if you add the *binary* values 1 and 1, you must carry a 1 into the "twos" column to produce the correct result (10).

The addition gets slightly more complicated when you add multi-bit numbers, and have to include a carry from a previous column. To illustrate, this operation involves two carries:

```
  1011
+   11
  1110
```

The addition of the rightmost column (1+1) produces a result of 0 and a carry of 1 into the second column. With the carry, the addition of the second column (1+1+1) produces a result of 1 and a carry into the third column.

The general rules for binary addition are shown in this table:

Inputs			Results	
Operand #1	Operand #2	Carry	Sum	Carry
0	0	0	0	0
0	1	0	1	0
1	0	0	1	0
1	1	0	0	1
0	0	1	1	0
0	1	1	0	1
1	0	1	0	1
1	1	1	1	1

Signed Numbers

Until now, we have been discussing how to represent *unsigned numbers* in binary. As we mentioned earlier, each bit in an unsigned number has a weight that reflects its position. The rightmost (or least-significant) bit has a weight of 1 and each more-significant bit has a weight twice that of its predecessor. Therefore, if all 8 bits in a byte are 0, the byte has the value 0; if they are all 1, the byte has a value 255.

Many of your calculations, however, will involve positive or negative values, that is, *signed numbers*. When a byte contains a signed number, only the seven least-significant bits (0 through 6) represent data; the most-significant bit (7) specifies the sign of the number. *The sign bit is 0 if the number is positive or zero and 1 if it is negative.* Figure 0–2 shows the arrangement of signed and unsigned bytes.

When holding a signed number, a single byte can represent positive values between 0 (binary 00000000) and +127 (binary 01111111) and negative values between −1 (binary 11111111) and −128 (binary 10000000).

Twos-Complement Representation

Why is −1 represented in binary as 11111111, instead of as 10000000? The answer is that negative signed numbers are represented in their *twos-complement form*. Computer scientists invented the twos-complement form to eliminate the problems associated with letting zero have two different values, all 0s ("positive zero") and all 0s with a 1 in the sign position ("negative zero").

To find the binary representation of a negative number (that is, to find its twos-complement form), simply take the positive form of the number and reverse each bit—change each 1 to a 0 and each 0 to a 1—then add 1 to the result. The following example shows how to calculate

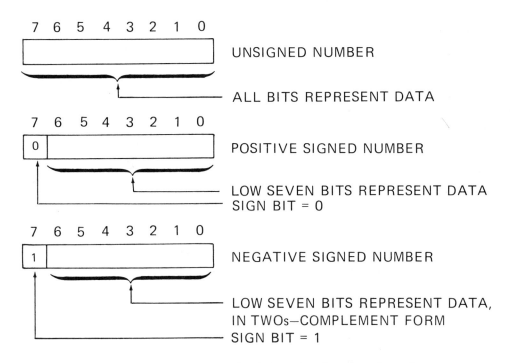

Figure 0–2. Representation of signed and unsigned numbers.

the twos-complement binary representation of -32:

```
  00100000   +32
  11011111   Reverse all bits
+        1   Add 1
  11100000   twos-complement
```

Of course, the twos-complement convention makes negative numbers difficult to decipher. Fortunately, you can use the same procedure we just gave to find the positive form of a (twos-complemented) negative number. For example, to find what value 11010000 has, proceed as follows:

```
  00101111   Reverse all bits
+        1   Add 1
  00110000   = 16 + 32 = +48
```

Assembler programs let you enter numbers in decimal form (signed or unsigned), and automatically do all converting. You may occasionally want to interpret a negative number, however, that is stored in memory or in a register, so you should know how to make these conversions yourself.

0.2 The Hexadecimal Numbering System

Although the binary numbering system is an accurate way to represent numbers in memory, strings of nothing but 1s and 0s are very difficult to work with. They are error-prone as well, because a number like 10110101 is extremely easy to mistype.

Years ago, programmers found that they were generally operating on *groups* of bits, rather than individual bits. The earliest processors were 4-bit devices (they processed information 4 bits at a time), so the logical alternative to binary was a system that numbered bits in groups of four.

As you know, 4 bits can represent the binary values 0000 through 1111 (which is equivalent to the decimal values 0 through 15), a total of 16 possible combinations. If a numbering system is to represent those 16 combinations, it must have 16 digits. That is, it must be a *base 16* system.

If "binary" denotes the base 2 system and "decimal" denotes the base 10 system, what term is appropriate for a base 16 system? Well, whoever named the base 16 system combined the Greek word "hex" (for six) with the Latin word "decem" (for ten) to form the word hexadecimal. Hence, the base 16 system is called the *hexadecimal numbering system*.

Of the 16 digits in the hexadecimal numbering system, the first 10 are labeled 0 through 9 (decimal values 0 through 9) and the last six are

Table 0–1. Hexadecimal numbering system.

Hexadecimal Digit	Binary Value	Decimal Value	Hexadecimal Digit	Binary Value	Decimal Value
0	0000	0	8	1000	8
1	0001	1	9	1001	9
2	0010	2	A	1010	10
3	0011	3	B	1011	11
4	0100	4	C	1100	12
5	0101	5	D	1101	13
6	0110	6	E	1110	14
7	0111	7	F	1111	15

labeled A through F (decimal values 10 through 15). Table 0–1 lists the binary and decimal equivalents for each of the 16 hexadecimal digits.

Like binary and decimal digits, each hexadecimal digit has a weight that is some multiple of its base. Since the hexadecimal numbering system is based on 16, each hexadecimal digit has a weight 16 times greater than the digit to its immediate right. That is, the rightmost digit has a weight of 16^0, the next has a weight of 16^1, and so on. For example, the hexadecimal value 3AF has a decimal value of 943, because

$$(3 \times 16^2) + (A \times 16^1) + (F \times 16^0)$$

reduces to the decimal form

$$(3 \times 256) + (10 \times 16) + (15 \times 1) = 943$$

Uses of Hexadecimal Numbers

While BASIC and other high-level languages usually display numbers in decimal form, assembly language generally displays numbers in hexadecimal form. This includes addresses, instruction codes, and the contents of memory locations and registers. Therefore, to get maximum benefit from your programming, you should try to "think hexadecimal." Although this is difficult at first, it becomes easier as you gain more experience. To help you along, Appendix A provides tables for converting decimal numbers to hexadecimal, and vice versa.

Exercises (answers on page 205)

1. Convert the following decimal values to binary:
   (a) 12 (b) 17 (c) 45 (d) 72

2. Convert the following unsigned binary values to decimal:
   (a) 1000 (b) 10101 (c) 11111
3. How would you represent the three binary numbers in Exercise 2 in hexadecimal?
4. List the decimal equivalent of hexadecimal D8 if:
   (a) D8 represents an unsigned number
   (b) D8 represents a signed number

1

Introduction to Assembly Language Programming

1.1 What is Assembly Language?

Like BASIC, assembly language is a set of words that tell the computer what to do. The words in the assembly language instruction set, however, refer to computer components directly. It's like the difference between telling someone to walk down to the corner and telling him precisely how to move his muscles and maneuver past obstacles. Obviously, a simple command is sufficient most of the time; only athletes or mountain climbers need the more detailed instructions.

Assembly language programs give the computer detailed commands, such as "load 32 into the AX register," "transfer the contents of the CL register into the DL register," and "store the number in the DL register into memory location 3,456." As you see, BASIC and assembly language differ in how you instruct the computer. *With BASIC, you speak in generalities; with assembly language, you speak in specifics.*

Although assembly language programs take more time and effort to write than BASIC programs, they also run much faster. The level of detail is the key here. The idea is the same as an athlete who runs faster or jumps farther by watching every step of what he or she does. Precise form is essential to achieving maximum performance.

Because assembly language requires you to operate on the computer's internal components, you must understand the features and capabilities of the integrated circuit (or "chip") that holds these components, the computer's microprocessor. In this book, we will study two popular microprocessors: the *8086* and the *8088*. Before getting into the details of these chips, however, we should take a brief look at how they came into being.

1.2 Evolution of the 8086 and 8088

The earliest microprocessors were 4-bit devices. This means they could transfer only 4 bits of information at a time. To transfer more than 4 bits, these microprocessors had to make several separate transfer operations. Of course, this also made them slow.

The Intel 8008, introduced in 1972, was the first commercial *8-bit* microprocessor (it transferred information 8 bits at a time), and is still considered the foremost "first-generation" 8-bit microprocessor. Designed with a calculator-like architecture, the 8008 had an accumulator, six scratchpad registers, a stack pointer (a special address register for temporary storage), eight address registers, and special instructions to perform input and output. In 1973, Intel introduced a "second-generation" version of the 8008, and called it the 8080.

The 8080 is an upgraded 8008; it has more addressing and I/O capability and more instructions, and executes instructions faster. The internal organization is better, too, although Intel maintained the overall 8008 architectural philosophy in the 8080. The 8080 is historically the de facto standard in second-generation microprocessors—the device many people still think of first when someone mentions microprocessors.

By 1976, advances in technology allowed Intel to produce an enhanced version of the 8080, called the 8085. Essentially a repackaged 8080, the 8085 added such features as an on-chip oscillator, power-on reset (to initialize the microprocessor), vectored interrupts (to service the needs of peripherals), a serial I/O port (to attach printers and other peripherals), and a single, +5-volt power supply (the 8080 requires two supplies).

By the time the 8085 was introduced, Intel had heavy competition in the 8-bit microprocessor marketplace. Zilog Corporation's 8080 enhancement, the Z80, was catching on, as were non-8080 designs such as the Motorola 6800 and the MOS Technology (now Commodore) 6502. Rather than continue the struggle on the now-diluted 8-bit front, Intel made a quantum leap forward in 1978 by introducing the 8086, a *16-bit* microprocessor that can process data ten times as fast as the 8080.

The 8086 is software-compatible with the 8080 at the assembly language level. This means that with some minimal translation, existing 8080 programs can be reassembled and executed on the 8086. To allow for this, the 8080 registers and instruction set appear as subsets of the 8086 registers and instructions. With this compatibility, Intel could capitalize on its experience with the 8080 to gain acceptance in more sophisticated applications.

In the same vein, realizing that many designers will still want to use the cheaper 8-bit support and peripheral chips in their 16-bit systems, Intel produced a version of the 8086 with the same 16-bit internal data paths, but with an *8-bit data bus* coming out of the chip. This microprocessor, the 8088, is identical to the 8086, except the 8088 takes more time to make 16-bit transfers because it must perform them with two separate 8-bit transfers. Even so, for applications that deal primarily with 8-bit rather than 16-bit quantities, the 8088 can approach to within 10 percent of the 8086's processing power!

Since speed is the only difference between the 8086 and the 8088, most of the material in this book applies to both microprocessors. That is, you can run every program we list on either an 8086-based computer or an 8088-based computer. Of course, where speed is involved, we will tell you how the microprocessors differ.

To save you the trouble of reading "8086/8088" throughout the book, we will refer to both microprocessors by the generic term 8086. Whenever you see "8086," you should mentally convert it to "8086 and 8088" unless you are told otherwise. (Incidentally, Intel literature usually refers to the 8086 and the 8088 as the iAPX 86 and the iAPX 88, respectively, so you may encounter those names as well.)

With this prologue aside, we can now take a look at the features of the 8086. Again, they also apply to the 8088.

1.3 Overview of the 8086 Microprocessor

Internally, the 8086 holds information in a group of 16-bit boxes called "registers." It has 14 registers in all: 12 data and address registers, plus an instruction pointer (the program-addressing register) and a status (or "flags") register. The 12 data and address registers can be divided into three groups of four registers, called *data registers, pointer and index registers,* and *segment registers.*

Addressing

Since the 8086's instruction pointer and address registers are 16 bits wide, you would expect it to address no more than 64K bytes (65,536 bytes) of memory—the standard addressing range of 8-bit microprocessors. The 8086, however, always generates a 20-*bit address*; it does this by adding a 16-bit offset to the contents of a segment register multiplied by 16. That is:

Physical Address = Offset Address + (16 × Segment Register)

In reality, the 8086 doesn't actually *multiply* the segment register by 16, but instead uses it as if it had four extra zero bits (see Figure 1–1). Adding zeros to the end is the same as multiplying, however, because each time a binary number is displaced one bit position to the left, its value is doubled. Thus, displacing the segment register *four* bit positions to the left "multiplies" its contents by 16, since $2 \times 2 \times 2 \times 2 = 16$.

For example, if the offset address has the value 10H—where the H suffix means hexadecimal—and the segment register contains 2000H,

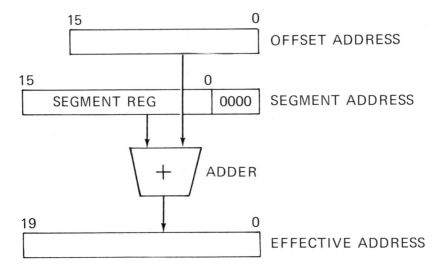

Figure 1–1. How a 20-bit address is generated.

the 8086 calculates the physical address as follows (operands are shown in binary form):

```
         0000 0000 0001 0000       Offset address
 +0010 0000 0000 0000 0000       Segment address
   0010 0000 0000 0001 0000       Physical address
```

Therefore, the memory location referenced here has the 20-bit address 20010H.

With a 20-bit address at its disposal, the 8086 can access any of 1,048,576 bytes. (We refer to this value as *1 megabyte*, but you may think of it as 1,024K bytes, if you like.) That's 16 times the addressing range of the 8080!

Segments and Offsets

With most microprocessors, you reference a memory location by supplying a single number, but with the 8086, each memory reference requires two terms: a segment number and an offset. The reason for this odd addressing scheme is that the 8086 requires program instructions and data to be in separate parts of memory, that is, in different segments. Therefore, if you want to address a data location, for example, the 8086 needs the address of the beginning of the data segment (from the data segment register) and the position of the desired location within that segment (its offset).

Think of the way you find someone's house in a city. First, you drive to the street where he lives (that could be considered his segment number), then proceed to his address along that street (his offset).

Fortunately, you generally provide only the offset and let the 8086 supply the segment number. We discuss this point in more detail later in the book.

Software Features

The software features of the 8086 are impressive by any standard, but will be especially welcomed by programmers who struggled with the earlier 8-bit microprocessors. The 8086 can perform arithmetic operations on signed or unsigned binary numbers of either 8 bits or 16 bits, and on decimal numbers stored in either "packed" (two digits per byte) or "unpacked" (one digit per byte) form. It can also operate on character strings of either bytes or words up to 64K bytes long.

The 8086 instruction set has 92 basic instruction types and provides seven different addressing modes for accessing data. The combination of the instruction types, the addressing modes (each with a variety of operand combinations), and the various data types we just mentioned gives the 8086 *thousands* of possible instructions to execute. In fact, the combined power of these features allows the 8086 to deliver twice the performance of an 8085, if both processors are driven at the same speed.

Measuring Speed

Like electronic watches, microprocessors are powered by quartz crystals. The crystal sends out pulses at a steady, fixed rate, which determines how fast the microprocessor operates. In most 8086- or 8088-based computers, the crystal emits about five million pulses per second.

Computerists don't refer to pulses per second, however, but to *cycles per second*, or *hertz*. Pulses per second, cycles per second, and hertz all mean the same thing, but in this book we will use the term hertz (or, more often, the abbreviation Hz). For example, the crystal in the IBM Personal Computer—and all other computers that claim to be compatible with the PC—operates an 8088 at 4,770,000 cycles per second; we therefore say that the PC has a 4.77-MHz clock.

Since this book describes the 8086 and 8088 microprocessors rather than a specific computer, we can't tell you how fast an instruction will run on your particular computer. Nevertheless, every 8086 instruction takes a certain number of *clock cycles* to run, and we do know those numbers. For example, we know the 8086 takes three clock cycles to execute an add instruction.

To find out how much real time an instruction takes to execute on your computer, you determine the duration of a clock cycle, then multiply that duration by the number of clock cycles. To find the duration, divide the clock speed in megahertz (MHz) into 1.

For example, if your computer has a 5-MHz clock, each clock cycle takes 200×10^{-9} seconds ($\frac{1}{5,000,000}$ seconds), or 200 *nanoseconds*. (A nanosecond, abbreviated ns, is one billionth of a second, or 10^{-9} seconds.) Thus, an add instruction will take 600 ns to execute (three cycles per instruction times 200 ns per cycle). Throughout this book we will give the clock cycle times for various instructions. To convert these values to real time for your computer, use the procedure we just gave. That is,

Time in nanoseconds = Clocks/(Speed in hertz)

The fastest instructions—for example, one that copies the contents of one register into another—execute in two cycles, or 400 ns at 5 MHz. The slowest instruction, a signed 16-bit by 16-bit division, can take up to 206 clock cycles, or about 41 microseconds at 5 MHz, to execute. (A microsecond, abbreviated μs, is one millionth of a second, also expressed as 10^{-6} seconds or 1,000 ns.) As you can see, even this "slowest" instruction executes in the remarkable time of 0.000041 second!

Input/Output Space

In addition to its 1-megabyte memory space, the 8086 can address external devices through 64K I/O ports—that is, 65,536 ports. There are input and output instructions that let you communicate with the first 256 ports (0 through 255) directly. Other instructions let you access any of the 64K I/O ports *indirectly*, by putting its identifying number (0 through 65535) in a data register. Like locations in memory, any port may be 8 or 16 bits wide.

Memory Allocation

Most of the 1-megabyte address space is available for system and user programs, but the 8086 uses some of the highest and lowest locations for special purposes. The highest 16 bytes of memory hold one or more system reset instructions. The 8086 automatically executes these instructions when you turn on the power. The lowest 1,024 bytes of memory hold the addresses of programs the 8086 executes when an external device interrupts it.

Interrupts

We are all confronted with interruptions from time to time. Some are pleasant, some are unpleasant, and some are neutral. You can ignore some interruptions, if you like; a telephone or doorbell ringing, perhaps, or a child tugging at your sleeve. (On second thought, it's practically impossible to ignore the child!) You simply can't ignore other kinds of interruptions, such as getting a flat tire on the expressway; you must deal with them as soon as possible.

Whatever their cause, interruptions are essentially requests for our attention. In the same way, peripherals in a computer system can request the attention of the processor. The event that makes a processor stop executing its program to perform some requested activity is called an *interrupt*.

Interrupts increase the overall efficiency of a computer system, because they let external devices request the attention of the processor as needed. If a system had no interrupts, the processor would have to *poll* every device in the system periodically, to see if any of them required attention. This would be like having a telephone with no bell. You would have to pick up the receiver every so often just to find out whether anyone is on the line!

The 8086 can process two kinds of interrupts: those it can ignore and those it must service as soon as they occur. Interrupts can be generated by external devices, such as disks and other high-speed peripherals; internally, by interrupt-generating instructions; or, under certain conditions, by the 8086 itself.

Types of Interrupts

The 8086 can recognize 256 different interrupts, each with a unique *type code* that identifies it to the microprocessor. The 8086 uses this type code (a number between 0 and 255) to point to a location in an *interrupt vector table* in memory, which contains the address of the routine that handles the interrupt.

Of the 256 possible interrupt types, five are allocated to internal interrupts. These are:

- *Type 0, divide error,* occurs if a divide instruction produces a quotient that is too large to be contained in the result register, or if you attempt to divide by zero.
- *Type 1, single-step,* occurs after every instruction when the 8086 is operating in its "single-step" debugging mode.
- *Type 2, nonmaskable interrupt,* is a type of interrupt that cannot be "locked out" under program control, as all other interrupt types can. Type 2 interrupts generally inform the processor of some catastrophic event, such as imminent loss of power.
- *Type 3, interrupt instruction,* is a special 1-byte instruction that is used to set up "breakpoints" (stopping points) in software debugging programs.
- *Type 4, overflow,* is triggered by a special interrupt instruction (INTO) if a previous operation has produced an "overflow" condition. Overflow is discussed in Section 1.4.

Besides these five internal interrupt types, the 8086 provides 251 unassigned types that are available for additional interrupts, either internal or external.

Buses and Other Lines on the Chip

Both the 8086 and the 8088 are packaged as a 40-pin integrated circuit, or "chip." Memory addresses come out of the chip on a *20-line address bus*. In the 8086, the first 16 lines of the address bus are also used to transfer data into and out of the microprocessor; they form its *16-bit data bus*. Similarly, the first eight lines of the 8088's address bus form its *8-bit data bus*. Thus, we say the address bus and the data bus are "multiplexed." The four high-order address lines are also multiplexed; they carry status information during memory and I/O operations.

The 8086 and 8088 operate from a 5-volt power supply, and have one pin for power and two pins for ground. Since the processor also needs a clock (5 MHz is standard), one more pin accepts the clock input. The remaining 16 pins on the chip carry *control signals*, which we discuss later.

1.4 The 8086's Internal Registers

Since this book is devoted primarily to programming the 8086, the most logical place to begin is by discussing the internal registers at your disposal. Figure 1–2 shows the three groups of data and address registers, the 16-bit Instruction Pointer (IP), and the 16-bit Flags register.

Data Registers

You may treat the data registers as either four 16-bit registers or eight 8-bit registers, depending on whether you are operating on 16-bit words or 8-bit bytes. The 16-bit registers are named AX, BX, CX, and DX. Within these "X" registers are 8-bit registers named AL, AH, BL, BH, CL, CH, DL, and DH; here, the L and H suffixes identify the low-order and high-order bytes of the 16-bit registers. For example, AL and AH hold the low and high bytes, repectively, of AX.

All of these data registers are available for general programming use, but certain instructions also use them implicitly. Specifically:

- *AX, the Accumulator,* is used in word-size multiplication, division, and I/O operations, and in some string operations. The *AL register* is used in the byte-size counterparts of these same operations, and in translate and decimal arithmetic operations. The *AH register* is also used in byte-size multiplications and divisions.

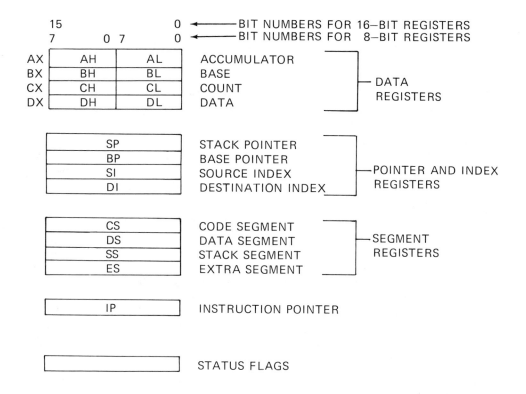

Figure 1–2. Programmable registers within the 8086.

- *BX, the Base register,* is heavily used to address data in memory.
- *CX, the Count register,* acts as a repetition counter for loop operations and as an element counter for string operations. The *CL register* holds the shift count for multiple-bit shift and rotate operations.
- *DX, the Data register,* is used in word-size multiplication and division operations. It can also provide the port number in I/O operations.

Former 8080 or 8085 programmers will note that AH is the only data register unique to the 8086; the others are relabeled 8080/8085 registers. In the 8080, AL is called A and BX, CX, and DX are called HL, BC, and DE, respectively.

The data registers are the only ones you may reference as either 8- or 16-bit. The registers in the remaining groups are exclusively 16-bit registers.

Segment Registers

As we mentioned earlier, 8086- and 8088-based computers keep programs and data in separate areas of memory. These program and data areas, which can be up to 64K bytes long, are called "segments." The

8086 can work with up to four segments at a time; it holds the starting address of these segments in four *segment registers*. The functions of these four registers are:

- The *code segment (CS) register* points to the segment that holds the program currently being executed. The 8086 combines the contents of CS (multiplied by 16) with the contents of the instruction pointer (IP) to calculate the memory address of its next instruction.
- The *stack segment (SS) register* points to the current stack segment. A stack is a data structure in memory that functions as a temporary depository for data and addresses. The 8088 uses the stack to hold a return address while a subroutine is being executed, but you may also use it to preserve the contents of registers that a subroutine alters. We will say more about stacks later.
- The *data segment (DS) register* points to the curent data segment, which usually holds variables.
- The *extra segment (ES) register* points to the current "extra" segment, which is used in string operations.

In large systems, the four segments may lie in different parts of memory. In systems that have no more than 64K bytes of memory, the segments often overlap.

Pointer and Index Registers

Just as the 8086 combines a base address in CS with an offset in IP to calculate the address of an instruction in the code segment, it accesses data in other segments by combining a base address in a segment register with an offset in another register. To access the stack segment, the 8086 gets the base address from SS and the offset from one of the *pointer registers (SP or BP)*. To access the data segment, it gets the base address from DS and the offset from BX, or from one of the *index registers (SI or DI)*. It can also access the extra segment by using a base address from ES, which we discuss further in Chapter 2.

Instruction Pointer

Most microprocessors execute a program by fetching an instruction from memory, executing it, then fetching the next instruction, and so on. This naturally introduces some delay, because the microprocessor must wait until each new instruction has been fetched from memory before execution can begin. The 8086 eliminates much of this delay by assigning these two tasks—fetching instructions and executing instructions—to separate, special-purpose units within the chip.

One of these, the Bus Interface Unit (BIU), fetches instructions from

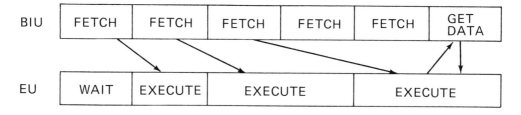

Figure 1–3. Parallel operation in the "pipelined" 8086.

memory and passes data between the execution hardware and the "outside world." The other, the Execution Unit (EU), only executes instructions. Because these units are independent, the BIU can fetch a new instruction from memory at the same time the EU is executing a previously-fetched instruction.

Whenever the BIU fetches an instruction, it adds that instruction to a *pipeline* within the microprocessor. Thus, when the EU finishes executing a given instruction, it can usually find the next instruction in the pipeline.

Since the BIU cannot know the sequence in which the program will execute, it always fetches instructions from consecutive memory locations. Therefore, the only time the EU must wait for an instruction to be fetched is when program execution transfers to a new, nonsequential address. When that happens, the EU must wait for the BIU to clear the pipeline and fetch the next instruction. Then, and only then, the 8086 waits like most other microprocessors wait for *every* instruction to be fetched. Figure 1–3 shows parallel fetching and executing in the 8086.

Because the 8086 works in this rather unique way, the people at Intel chose to differentiate their "next execution address" register from other manufacturers' "next fetch address" register by calling it an *instruction pointer (IP)* instead of a program counter (PC). The IP always contains the offset of the instruction the 8086's EU will execute next. Because the IP has this one dedicated purpose, you cannot perform arithmetic on its contents. The 8086, however, has instructions that change the IP and other instructions that transfer its contents to and from the stack.

Flags

You will often want your program to make a "decision" based on the result of the instruction the 8086 just executed. For example, you may want to do one thing if an addition yields zero (perhaps print "Balance is zero!" in an accounting program) and something entirely different if the result is not zero.

The 16-bit *Flags register* reports various status conditions that help your program make decisions. Six bits hold statuses; three others let you control the 8086 from within a program.

Figure 1–4 shows how these nine "flags" are arranged in the Flags

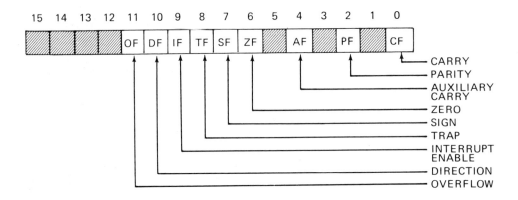

Figure 1–4. The Flags register.

register. The flags operate as follows:

1. *Bit 0, the Carry Flag (CF)*, is 1 if an add operation produces a carry or a subtract operation produces a borrow; otherwise, it is 0. CF also holds the value of a bit that has been shifted or rotated out of a register or memory location, and reflects the result of a compare operation. Finally, CF also acts as a result indicator for multiplications; see the description of bit 11 (OF) for details.

2. *Bit 2, the Parity Flag (PF)*, is 1 if the result of an operation has an even number of 1 bits; otherwise, it is 0. PF is primarily used in data communications applications.

3. *Bit 4, the Auxiliary Carry Flag (AF)*, is similar to the CF bit, except AF reflects the presence of a carry or borrow out of bit 3. CF is useful for operating on "packed" decimal numbers.

4. *Bit 6, the Zero Flag (ZF)*, is 1 if the result of an operation is zero; a nonzero result clears ZF to 0.

5. *Bit 7, the Sign Flag (SF)*, is meaningful only during operations on signed numbers. SF is 1 if an arithmetic, logical, shift, or rotate operation produces a negative result; otherwise, it is 0. In other words, SF reflects the most-significant (sign) bit of the result, regardless of whether the result is 8 or 16 bits long.

6. *Bit 8, the Trap Flag (TF)*, makes the 8086 "single-step" through a program, for debugging purposes.

7. *Bit 9, the Interrupt Enable Flag (IF)*, allows the 8086 to recognize interrupt requests from external devices in the system. Clearing IF to 0 makes the 8086 ignore interrupt requests until IF becomes 1.

8. *Bit 10, the Direction Flag (DF)*, makes the 8086 automatically decrement (DF = 1) or increment (DF = 0) the index register(s) after executing a string instruction. When DF is 0, the 8086 progresses forward through a string (toward higher addresses, or "right to left"). When DF is 1, it progresses backward through a string (toward lower addresses, or "left to right").

9. *Bit 11, the Overflow Flag (OF),* is primarily an error indicator during operations on signed numbers. OF is 1 if the addition of two like-signed numbers, or the subtraction of two opposite-signed numbers, produces a result that exceeds the capacity of the operand; otherwise, it is 0.

OF is also 1 if the most-significant (sign) bit of the operand changed at any time during an arithmetic shift operation; otherwise, it is 0.

The OF flag, in combination with the CF flag, also indicates the length of a multiplication result. If the upper half of the product is nonzero, OF and CF are 1; otherwise, both bits are 0.

Finally, OF is 1 if the quotient produced by a divide operation overflows the result register.

The shaded bit positions in Figure 1–4 (1, 3, 5, and 12 through 15) are unused. If you ever read the status of the Flags register, these bits will be 0.

Don't make the mistake of assuming that the flags are in one state or another at any given time. The 8086 has instructions that let you set or reset flags as you choose. When in doubt, *use* these instructions.

The 8086 has conditional transfer instructions that test the state of the Carry (CF), Parity (PF), Zero (ZF), Sign (SF), and Overflow (OF) flags, and cause program execution to continue inline or at some other location in memory, depending on the result of the test.

Exercises (answers on page 205)

1. How does the instruction set of the 8088 differ from that of the 8086?
2. What physical address does the 8086 generate when you combine an offset value of 2H with a segment register containing 4000H?
3. If the AX register contains 1A2BH, what does AL contain?
4. Which segment register normally accesses variables in your programs?
5. Which bit in the Flags register tells whether a preceding subtract operation produced a negative result?

2

Using an Assembler

2.1 Introducing the Assembler

In Chapter 1 you learned that assembly language lets you write programs at the level the microprocessor understands, but doesn't force you to memorize a set of numeric codes. Instead, you write your instructions as English-like abbreviations, then run an *assembler* program to convert the abbreviations to their numeric equivalents.

By convention, the program written with abbreviations is called the "source program" and the numeric, microprocessor-compatible form of this program is called the "object program." Hence, the assembler's job is to convert source programs *you* can understand into object programs the *microprocessor* can understand.

Intel calls the 8086/8088 assembly langage *ASM-86*. In this chapter we will describe the features of ASM-86 assemblers. You may own an assembler that has more features, or fewer, but if it is compatible with ASM-86 (which most are), our descriptions will apply.

2.2 Developing an Assembly Language Program

Although assembly language programs look quite different from BASIC programs, you follow the same procedures to develop them. In assembly language, however, the *mechanics* are more involved. There are six steps in developing an assembly language program:

1. Define the task and the program. This often requires you to draw a *flowchart*, a "blueprint" of how the program operates.
2. Write the program instructions on paper.
3. Type the written program into the computer, using an *editor*.

4. Assemble the program. If the assembler finds errors, correct them with the editor and re-assemble the program.
5. Execute (run) the program.
6. Check the results. If they differ from what you expected, you must find the errors or "bugs"; that is, you must "debug" the program.

If your program is short and simple, you should be able to perform most of these steps quickly. Longer and more complex programs, however, will require more time on each step, especially in defining the problem itself. These steps are illustrated in a sample program at the end of this chapter, to help you learn the ground rules and mechanics of developing programs.

Editor

Step 3 refers to an *editor*. This is a program that lets you enter and prepare your program. We call your readable version of the program the *source program*.

Assembler

The computer cannot directly execute the program you prepare using the editor. An assembler must convert that source program into an *object program* the computer can understand.

Some assemblers require you to specify where you want the object program stored in memory; others (called *relocating* assemblers) can automatically store it at any convenient place.

Most assemblers also allow you to develop a set of subprograms (or *modules*), which you eventually link together to form the final program. The linking process would follow step 4 in our preceding list.

2.3 Source Statements

Having considered the general approach to developing a program, we can finally look at what it contains. The program you write—the *source program*—is a sequence of *statements* that tell the microprocessor what to do. A source statement (a line in your program) can be either an assembly language instruction or an assembler directive.

Assembly language instructions are symbolic representations of the 8086 microprocessor's instruction set. Some manuals refer to these as "machine instructions," because they tell the "machine" (the 8086) what to do. By contrast, *directives* (sometimes called pseudo operations, or simply "pseudo-ops") tell the *assembler* what to do.

Source statements of either kind can also include *operators*, which give the assembler information about an operand, where ambiguities exist. We discuss assembly language instructions, assembler directives, and operators in the sections that follow.

Constants in Source Statements

The ASM-86 assembler lets you enter constants in five different forms:

1. *Binary*—A sequence of 1's and 0's followed by the letter B; for example, 10111010B.
2. *Decimal*—A sequence of the digits 0 through 9; for example, 129.
3. *Hexadecimal*—A sequence of the digits 0 through 9 and the letters A through F, followed by the letter H. The first character must be a numeric digit (0 through 9); for example, 0E23H. Here, the 0 prefix tells the assembler that E23H is a *number*, rather than a symbol or a variable name.
4. *Octal*—A sequence of the digits 0 through 7, followed by the letter Q; for example, 1477Q. (The octal notation is rarely used these days, so you can probably ignore it.)
5. *Character*—A string of text characters enclosed in single quotes; for example, 'Message'.

It is also possible to specify a *negative* number. If the number is a decimal value, you simply precede it with a minus sign (for example, −10). If the number is a binary, hexadecimal, or octal value, you must enter the number in its "twos-complement" form. For example, 11100000B, 0E0H, and 340Q are alternate forms of decimal −32.

2.4 Assembly Language Instructions

Each assembly language instruction in a source program is composed of up to four *fields*, as follows:

```
[Label:] Mnemonic [Operand] [;Comment]
```

Of these, only the mnemonic field is always required. The label and comment fields are always optional; you may include or omit them at your discretion. The operand field applies only to instructions that *require* an operand; otherwise, you must omit it. (The brackets around the label, operand, and comment fields means they are optional; *don't* type the brackets into your programs.)

You may enter these fields anywhere on a line, but you must separate them with at least one space. An assembly language instruction that uses all four fields is

```
GETCOUNT: MOV CX,DI ;Initialize Count
```

Here are the details on each of the four fields in an assembly language instruction.

Label Field

The label field assigns a symbolic *name* to an assembly language instruction. This lets other instructions reference the labeled instruction by name, rather than by its numeric location. Any assembly language instruction may be labeled, but labels usually identify the "target" of a jump or procedure (subroutine) call instruction.

A label name may be up to 31 characters long and must end with a colon (:). It may consist of:

- *Alphabetic letters:* A through Z
- *Numeric digits:* 0 through 9
- *special characters:* ? . @ _ $

The symbols AH, AL, AX, BH, BL, BX, BP, CH, CL, CX, CS, DH, DL, DX, DI, DS, ES, SI, and SP are register names, so you can't use them as labels. You can't use assembler mnemonics (listed in Chapter 3) as labels either.

You can't put a space in a label, but you can get the same effect by using an underscore character (_). For example, you could write the previous sample instruction as

```
GET_COUNT: MOV CX,DI  ;Initialize Count
```

Clearly, GET_COUNT is more readable than GETCOUNT.

Selecting Label Names

Because ASM-86 lets you use various combinations of letters, digits, and symbols, almost any label you can think of is acceptable. We recommend, however, the following label selection rules:

- Make the name as short as possible, while still being reasonable. Thus, MPH is preferable to MILES_PER_HOUR and CUR_YR is a reasonable abbreviation for CURRENT_YEAR.
- Make the name easy to type without errors. The usual typing problems are several identical letters in a row (such as HHHH) and similar-looking characters (such as the letter O and the number 0, letter I and number 1, and letter S and number 5). There is no reason to invite typing errors; most of us make enough of them anyway.
- Do not use labels that could be confused with each other. For example, avoid using things like XXXX and XXYX. There's no sense in tempting fate and Murphy's Law.

NEAR and FAR Labels

The 8086 has instructions that can make the processor jump from one place to another in a program. For example, the instruction

```
JMP GET_COUNT
```

makes the 8086 transfer control to the instruction stored at the location labeled GET_COUNT. (In the preceding example, GET_COUNT is the starting location of a MOV instruction.) Hence, JMP does what GOTO does in BASIC, except JMP works with a label rather than a line number; assembly language programs do not operate with line numbers.

The 8086 can make this transfer in two ways:

1. If the label is in the *same* code segment as the control-transfer instruction (JMP in this case), the 8086 must load only the offset of the label into the Instruction Pointer (IP); the Code Segment (CS) register can remain as is.
2. If the label is in a *different* code segment than the transfer instruction, the 8086 must load the label's offset into IP and its segment number into CS.

Obviously, the assembler must tell the 8086 which approach to take. It does this by assigning one of two *distance attributes*, NEAR or FAR, to the instruction label. When transferring to a NEAR instruction, the processor changes on IP (see 1 above); when transferring to a FAR instruction, it changes both IP and CS (see 2).

The assembler makes *every* instruction NEAR unless you tell it otherwise. For example, in the instruction

```
GET_COUNT: MOV CX,DI
```

the label GET_COUNT has a NEAR attribute.

If your programs are typical, you may never need to jump to an instruction in another segment. If you do need to jump, however, you must give the instruction a label that has a FAR attribute. The easiest way to do this is with an EQU directive, like this:

```
FAR_START EQU FAR PTR START
START:    MOV CX,DI
```

Here, the MOV instruction has two labels: the NEAR label START and the FAR label FAR_START.

Mnemonic Field

The mnemonic field (the leading "m" is silent in mnemonic) holds the two- to six-letter acronym for the microprocessor instruction. For example, MOV is the acronym for a move instruction and ADD is the acronym for an add instruction. The assembler uses an internal conversion table to translate each acronym, or *mnemonic*, in the program into its numeric equivalent.

In addition to the mnemonic, many 8086 instructions require you to specify either one or two operands. The mnemonic tells the assembler how many operands, and which types of operands, to obtain from the operand field. The legal mnemonics are described in Chapter 3, so we will not list them here.

Operand Field

This field tells the 8086 where to find the data to be operated on. For example, in this move instruction:

```
MOV CX,DX
```

the operand *CX,DX* tells the 8086 to copy the contents of the DX register into the CX register.

The operand field is mandatory with some instructions and prohibited with others. If present, the operand field will contain either one or two operands, separated from the mnemonic by at least one space. If two operands are required, you must put a comma between them, as we did in the preceding example.

If an instruction has two operands, the first operand is the *destination* and the second operand is the *source*. The source operand refers to the value that will be added to, subtracted from, compared to, or copied into the destination operand. (In the preceding MOV example, source operand DX is copied into destination operand CX.) The source operand is never altered by the operation, but the destination operand is nearly always altered. In Chapter 3 we will discuss the addressing characteristics for each instruction in the 8086's instruction set.

Comment Field

This optional field is like a REM in BASIC. It is used to describe a statement in the source program, to make the program easier to understand. Comments must be preceded with a semicolon (;) and separated from the preceding field by at least one space. The assembler ignores comments, but prints them when you list the program.

Comments should describe what is being done, and not just restate the instruction. For example,

```
MOV CX,0 ;Clear the count register
```

is more meaningful than

```
MOV CX,0 ;Move 0 into CX
```

Stand-Alone Comments

You may also use comments by themselves, to describe a program or a portion of a program. To put a stand-alone comment in a program, enter a semicolon in column 1, then type the comment itself. The assembler will recognize the semicolon as the beginning of a comment line and ignore the rest of the line. For example,

```
;This line represents a stand-alone comment.
```

2.5 Assembler Directives

Directives tell the assembler (rather than the microprocessor) what to do. Directives can define symbols, reserve memory locations for variables, and perform a variety of other "housekeeping" tasks. Unlike assembly language instructions, most directives generate no object code.

Directive statements can have up to four fields:

```
[Name] Directive [Operand] [;Comment]
```

As the brackets show, only the directive field is always required. A name is mandatory with some directives, prohibited with others, and optional with the rest. The same applies to an operand. The comment field is always optional.

As with assembly language instructions, directive fields can be placed anywhere on a line, but they must be separated by at least one space.

Table 2–1 divides ASM-86's directives into five groups: data, segment and procedure, block specification, assembly control, and program linkage.

Data Directives

Data directives (Table 2–2) set up constants and variables for use in your programs.

EQU lets you assign a symbolic name to a constant value (16 bits maximum), another symbolic name, or an expression that evaluates as a constant. EQU is, then, the assembly language equivalent of the LET statement in BASIC. Examples of EQU are:

```
K         EQU 1024   ;A constant value
```

```
SPEED    EQU RATE    ;Another symbolic name
KMINUS1  EQU K-1     ;An expression
```

Most programs use locations in memory to hold *variables*—named data items you can change as needed. The assembler has three directives that define variables. *Define Byte* (*DB*) defines variables that are 8 bits long, while *Define Word* (*DW*) and *Define Doubleword* (*DD*) define variables that are 16 or 32 bits long. When defining a variable, you can either give it a specific value or simply *reserve* the space for later use by the program.

The data definition directives have the general formats

```
[name] DB expression[,...]
[name] DW expression[,...]
[name] DD expression[,...]
```

The operand *expression* can take any of several forms, depending on how you wish to define the variable. For instance, the expression may be a *constant*. The following statements show the allowable maximum and minimum values for byte- and word-size variables, in decimal:

```
BU_MAX DB 255    (maximum byte constant, unsigned)

BS_MAX DB 127    (maximum byte constant, signed)
```

Table 2–1. ASM–86 assembler directives.

Data
> DB
> DW
> DD
> EQU

Segment and Procedure
> ASSUME
> PROC/ENDP
> SEGMENT/ENDS

Block Specification
> GROUP
> NAME

Assembly Control
> END
> ORG

Program Linkage
> EXTRN
> PUBLIC

Table 2–2. Data directives.

Directive	Function
EQU	Format: `name EQU expression` Assigns value of *expression* to *name*.
DB	Format: `[name] DB expression[,...]` Defines a variable or allocates bytes of storage.
DW	Format: `[name] DW expression[,...]` Similar to DB, but allocates 2-byte words.
DD	Format: `[name] DD expression[,...]` Allocates 4-byte doublewords.

```
BS_MIN DB -128      (minimum byte constant, signed)

WU_MAX DW 65535     (maximum word constant, unsigned)

WS_MAX DW 32767     (maximum word constant, signed)

WS_MIN DW -32768    (minimum word constant, signed)
```

You can also let the assembler calculate the value of a constant, if you like, as in this example:

```
MINS_PER_DAY DW 60*24
```

You may also use directives to set up a data table in memory. To do this, simply list the table elements and separate them with a comma. The following sequence sets up two 12-element tables, one composed of bytes and the other of words:

```
B_TABLE  DB 0,0,0,0,8,-13                    (byte table)
         DB -100,0,55,63,63,63

W_TABLE  DW 1025,567,-30222,0,90,-129 (word table)
         DW 17,645,26534,367,78,-17
```

Here, the elements are arranged as two lines of six values, but you may assign *any* number of variables with one directive, as long as you don't put more than 132 characters on a line.

Incidentally, note that the first four elements and the last three elements of B_TABLE have the same value (0 and 63, respectively). The assembler has a special operator, called DUP, that allows you to specify repeating operands without entering them individually. Using DUP, you can set up B_TABLE with the shorter statement

```
B_TABLE DB 4 DUP(0),8,-13,-100,0,55,3 DUP(63)
```

You may also define a variable without giving it an initial value, by putting a question mark (?) in the expression field. For example, the statements

```
HIGH_TEMP   DB  ?
AVG_WEIGHT DW  ?
```

reserve 3 bytes in memory (1 byte for HIGH_TEMP, 2 bytes for AVG_WEIGHT), but don't store anything in them. Remember, these locations are *not initialized* in any way! Don't make the mistake of assuming they contain 0, or any other specific value.

You may also reserve space for a table in a similar way. The statement

```
BUFFER DW 7,12,98 DUP(?)
```

allocates a block of 100 words (200 bytes) in memory, but initializes only the first two.

Define Byte (DB) also accepts a *character string* as an expression. This lets you store messages, table headers, and other text strings in memory. In this case, you must enclose the string in single quotes, as shown here:

```
POLITE_MSG  DB    'The number you have entered is
            DB    ' too large'
            DB    ' to be properly processed.
            DB    ' Please re-enter your data.'
RUDE_MSG    DB    'Try again, dummy!'
```

Variables are also used to hold *memory addresses* that can be referenced by instructions in your program. As you know, each address has two components: a segment number and an offset.

If a label lies in the *same* segment as the referencing instruction, you need to provide only its offset. This can be done with the DW directive. For example, the statement

```
HERE_NEAR DW HERE
```

assigns the 16-bit offset of the label HERE to the variable HERE_NEAR.

If a label lies in a *different segment* than the referencing instruction, the 8086 needs to know both its segment number and its offset. You can provide both components with a DD directive. For example, the statement

```
HERE_FAR DD HERE
```

puts the 16-bit offset and 16-bit segment number of the label HERE in the variable HERE_FAR.

Segment and Procedure Directives

Table 2–3 summarizes the segment and procedure directives.

The SEGMENT and ENDS directives partition the assembly language source program into segments. A program may have up to four kinds of segments: data, code, extra, and stack.

For example, a data segment may look like this:

```
DATASEG    SEGMENT          (start of data segment)
A          DB          ?
B          DB          ?
SQUARES    DB          1,4,9,16,25,36,49,64
DATASEG    ENDS             (end of data segment)
```

and a code segment may look like this:

```
PROGCODE   SEGMENT          (start of code segment)
           ..
           ..
           MOV         AX,BX
           MOV         CL,DH
           MOV         DI,CX
           ..
           ..
PROGCODE   ENDS             (end of code segment)
```

The words SEGMENT and ENDS merely mark the boundaries of a segment; they don't specify which *kind* of segment is being defined. A separate directive, ASSUME, informs the assembler which segment register a segment belongs to.

ASSUME has the general form

```
ASSUME seg-reg:seg-name[,...]
```

where *seg-reg* is either DS, CS, SS, or ES (for data, code, stack, or extra segment) and *seg-name* is the segment name assigned by the SEGMENT directive.

ASSUME helps the assembler translate labels in the program into addresses. It does this by telling the assembler which segment register

Table 2–3. Segment and procedure directives.

Directive	Function

SEGMENT	Format: `seg-name  SEGMENT  [align-type]`
	`[combine-type]`
	`['class']`
	
	`. .`
	`. .`
	`seg-name  ENDS`
	Defines the boundaries of a named segment. An ENDS statement marks the end of the segment.

ASSUME	Format: `ASSUME  seg-reg:seg-name[,...]`
	`or`
	`ASSUME    seg-reg:NOTHING[,...]`
	Tells the assembler which segment register a segment belongs to. *ASSUME NOTHING* cancels any previous ASSUME for the specified register.

PROC	Format: `name    PROC`
	`. .`
	`. .`
	`RET`
	`name    ENDP`
	Assigns a *name* to a sequence of assembler statements. Every PROC definition must end with an ENDP statement.

you plan to use to address those labels. We normally put the ASSUME immediately after the code segment's SEGMENT statement. Thus, for the preceding two-segment program, the code segment would have this form:

```
PROGCODE    SEGMENT
            ASSUME      CS:PROGCODE,DS:DATASEG
            MOV         AX,DATASEG
            MOV         DS,AX
            . .
            . .
            MOV         AX,BX
            MOV         CL,DH
            MOV         CS,DI
            . .
            . .
PROGCODE    ENDS
```

Here, ASSUME tells the assembler "whenever you find a label in the PROGCODE segment, use the segment number in CS to calculate its address" and, similarly, "whenever you find a label in DATASEG, use the segment number in DS to calculate its address." Note that we also load the data segment address into DS; the ASSUME does not take care of this.

The PROC and ENDP directives mark the beginning and end of a *procedure*—a block of instructions that can be executed from various places in a program. Whenever your program "calls" a procedure, the 8086 executes it, then returns to the place where the call took place. Because you write a procedure just once in a program, it frees you from typing the sequence each time you need it, and thereby makes your programs shorter.

Every procedure begins with a PROC directive and ends with an ENDP directive. If it also contains a RET (Return from Procedure) instruction, the procedure can be called a *subroutine*. RET causes the 8086 to resume at the point where the procedure was called. Finally, if you want to call a procedure a different code segment, you must precede it with a PUB-LIC directive.

A procedure always has one of two *distance* attributes: NEAR or FAR, as specified by the operand field. Omitting the operand makes the procedure NEAR. A NEAR procedure can be called only from within the segment in which it is defined, or from a segment that has the same ASSUME CS value. For example:

```
NEAR_NAME       PROC        NEAR
                . .
                . .
                RET
NEAR_NAME       ENDP
```

A FAR procedure can be called from any segment. For example:

```
                PUBLIC      FAR_NAME
FAR_NAME        PROC        FAR
                . .
                . .
                RET
FAR_NAME        ENDP
```

When the 8086 calls a procedure, it pushes a return address onto the stack. It will retrieve this address while it executes the RET instruction. If the procedure has a NEAR attribute, the call puts only an offset—the contents of the instruction pointer (IP)—on the stack. If the procedure has a FAR attribute, the call puts both a segment number—the contents of the code segment (CS) register—and an offset from IP on the stack, in that order.

When the program is assembled, the assembler translates each RET instruction into machine code that tells the 8086 how many return-address words to retrieve from the stack. A RET in a NEAR procedure makes it remove only one word (IP contents) from the stack, while a RET in a FAR procedure makes it remove two words (IP and CS contents).

Block Specification Directives

Table 2–4 summarizes the block specification directives.

The GROUP directive collects segments under one name, so they reside within a single 64K-byte block of memory. For example, if your program has a code segment (CODESEG) and a data segment (DATASEG), you could group them into a 64K block called CGROUP as follows:

```
CGROUP    GROUP     CODESEG,DATASEG
          ASSUME    CS:CGROUP,DS:CGROUP
DATASEG   SEGMENT
          ..
          ..
DATASEG   ENDS
CODESEG   SEGMENT
          ASSUME    CS:CODESEG,DS:DATASEG
          ..
          ..
CODESEG   ENDS
          END
```

The NAME directive assigns a name to a module. For example,

```
NAME THIS_MODULE
```

assigns the name THIS_MODULE to this module. Do not confuse this module name with a disk filename; it is stored *inside* the object module.

Assembly Control Directives

Table 2–5 summarizes the assembly control directives.
If you have a relocating assembler, you can simply let the computer

Table 2–4. Block specification directives.

Directive	Function
GROUP	Format: name GROUP seg-name[,...] Collects the specified segments under one name, so they all reside within a 64K-byte physical segment.
NAME	Format: NAME module-name Assigns a name to a module.

Table 2–5. Assembly control directives.

Directive	Function
ORG	Format: `ORG expression` Sets location counter to the address produced by *expression*. Assembler will store subsequent object code starting at that address.
END	Format: `END [expression]` Marks the end of the source program.

store your program's object code (instructions and data) in any convenient place in memory. If, however, your assembler does not have relocating capability, you must tell the computer where to store the object code. You do that with an ORG (origin) directive. For example,

```
ORG 120D
```

tells the computer to store the program's object code starting 120 bytes past the beginning of the code segment.

The END directive marks the end of the source program and tells the assembler where to stop assembling. Therefore, *END must be included in every source program.* Its general form is

```
END [expression]
```

where *expression*—usually a label—identifies the starting address of your source program. For example,

```
END MY_PROG
```

marks the end of the program MY_PROG.

The *expression* is optional if the program consists of only one source module, but mandatory if several modules must be linked to form the final run module. Using a label with END is always good documentation practice, however.

Program Linkage Directives

You may develop several independent subprograms (or *modules*) that you eventually link together to form your program. If any instructions in one module refer to labels in another module, you will need the directives defined in Table 2–6, PUBLIC and EXTRN.

The PUBLIC directive lists the symbols in this module that are referred to in other modules. A symbol can be a variable name or a label (in-

Table 2–6. Program linkage directives.

Directive	*Function*
PUBLIC	Format: `PUBLIC symbol[,...]` Makes the listed *symbol(s)* available to assembly modules that will be linked to this module.
EXTRN	Format: `EXTRN name:type[,...]` Specifies symbols that are defined in other assembly modules.

cluding PROC labels), but cannot be a name defined by an EQU directive.

EXTRN identifies the symbols in this module that are defined (and declared PUBLIC) in some other assembly module. EXTRN has the general form

```
EXTRN name:type[,...]
```

where *name* is the symbol defined in the other assembly module and *type* can be BYTE, WORD, DWORD, NEAR, FAR, ABS, or a name defined by an EQU directive.

For example, suppose you want to access the memory location TOTAL from two different modules. The module in which TOTAL is defined may include these statements:

```
        PUBLIC TOTAL
TOTAL DW      0        ;Make total = 0 to start
```

and the module in which TOTAL is referenced has this statement:

```
EXTRN TOTAL:WORD
```

2.6 Macros

Many assemblers also provide directives that let you create *macros*. A macro is a sequence of assembler statements (instructions and directives) that may appear several times in a program, with some optional modifications each time it is used.

As with procedures, the statements in the macro are preceded with a directive (usually CODEMACRO or simply MACRO) that gives the sequence a name and another directive (ENDM) that marks the end of the macro. Once a macro has been defined, you can use its name in your source program instead of the repeated instruction sequence.

Macros versus Procedures

Both macros and procedures provide a shorthand way to refer to a frequently-used instruction sequence, but they are not the same. A procedure appears once in a program, and the processor transfers to the procedure as needed. In contrast, the assembler *replaces* each occurrence of a macro name with the instructions that name represents. (Computer people say the assembler "expands" the macro.) Therefore, when you execute the program, the processor executes the macro instructions "in-line," without transferring elsewhere in memory, as it does with a procedure. Hence, *a macro name is a user-defined assembler directive*; it directs assembly rather than program execution.

Like procedures, macros make source programs shorter and easier to change. If you change the macro definition, the assembler incorporates the change for you every place the macro is used. Macros have a major disadvantage, however, that procedures do not have: since a macro gets expanded every time its name appears, it tends to make bulky machine language programs because it fills memory with repeated instruction sequences. Still, programmers often prefer macros for three reasons:

1. Macros are *dynamic*. You can easily modify the macro each time it is invoked, by changing its input parameters. You can pass parameters to procedures only in memory locations or registers, making procedures much more inflexible.
2. Macros make faster-executing programs, because the processor is not delayed by call and return instructions, as it is with procedures.
3. Macros can be entered into a *macro library* that programmers can draw from to create other programs.

A Simple Macro

The following macro adds the contents of two memory locations and stores the result in a third location:

```
%DEFINE(ADD_MEM(RESULT,LOC1,LOC2))(
        MOV         AX,LOC1
        ADD         AX,LOC2
        MOV         RESULT,AX)
```

With the ADD_MEM macro defined, the statement

```
%ADD_MEM(COST,PRICE,TAX)
```

in a source program tells the assembler to replace the word *ADD MEM* with the sequence

```
MOV         AX,PRICE
```

```
ADD        AX,TAX
MOV        COST,AX
```

This particular macro takes three parameters: a destination address and two operand addresses. If you specify fewer parameters than there are entries in the list (perhaps you omit TAX in our example), the assembler will either ignore any macro statements that use the unspecified entries or give an error message or a warning. Similarly, if you specify too many entries, the assembler will either ignore the excess parameters or give an error message or a warning.

2.7 Operators

An operator is a modifier used in the operand field of an assembly language statement or a directive statement. Table 2–7 divides the operators into five groups: arithmetic, logical, relational, value-returning, and attribute.

Arithmetic Operators

The assembler's arithmetic operators combine numeric operands and produce a numeric result. The most frequently used arithmetic operators are those that add (+), subtract (−), multiply (*), and divide (/).

A typical use of the addition operator is

```
TABLE_PLUS_2 DW TABLE+2
```

where the location TABLE_PLUS_2 receives the offset address of the second byte after the location TABLE (*not* the contents of TABLE plus 2).

Similarly, the subtraction operation

```
BYTE_DIFF DW TABLE1-TABLE
```

gives BYTE_DIFF the distance in bytes between TABLE1 and TABLE.

A typical use of the multiplication operator is

```
MINS_PER_DAY EQU 60*24
```

where you let the assembler calculate a value. Here, *MINS_PER_DAY* gets the value 1440.

The divide operator (/) returns the quotient produced by a divide operation. For example, the statement

```
PI_QUOT EQU 31416/10000
```

returns the value 3.

Table 2–7. Legal operators.

Operator	Function
Arithmetic	
+	Format: `value-1 + value-2` Adds value-1 and value-2.
–	Format: `value-1 - value-2` Subtracts value-2 from value -1.
*	Format: `value-1 * value-2` Multiplies value-2 by value-1.
/	Format: `value-1 / value-2` Divides value-1 by value-2, and returns the quotient.
MOD	Format: `value-1 MOD value-2` Divides value-1 by value-2, and returns the remainder.
SHL	Format: `value SHL expression` Shifts *value* left by *expression* bit positions.
SHR	Format: `value SHR expression` Shifts *value* right by *expression* bit positions.
Logical	
AND	Format: `value-1 AND value-2` Logically ANDs value-1 and value-2.
OR	Format: `value-1 OR value-2` Logically ORs value-1 and value-2.
XOR	Format: `value-1 XOR value-2` Logically exclusive-ORs value-1 and value-2.
NOT	Format: `NOT value` Reverses the state of each bit in *value*; that is, it takes the ones-complement of *value*.
Relational	
EQ	Format: `operand-1 EQ operand-2` True if the two operands are identical.
NE	Format: `operand-1 NE operand-2` True if the two operands are not identical.
LT	Format: `operand-1 LT operand-2` True if operand-1 is less than operand-2.
GT	Format: `operand-1 GT operand-2` True if operand-1 is greater than operand-2.
LE	Format: `operand-1 LE operand-2` True if operand-1 is less than or equal to operand-2.
GE	Format: `operand-1 GE operand-2` True if operand-1 is greater than or equal to operand-2.

Table 2–7. Legal operators (continued).

Operator	Function

Value-Returning
SEG
	Format: `SEG variable`
	              or
	              `SEG label`
	Returns the segment value of *variable* or *label*.

OFFSET	Format: `OFFSET variable`
	              or
	              `OFFSET label`
	Returns the offset value of *variable* or *label*.

TYPE	Format: `TYPE variable`
	              or
	              `TYPE label`
	If the operand is a variable, TYPE returns 1 (BYTE), 2 (WORD), or 4 (DOUBLEWORD). If the operand is a label, TYPE returns -1 (NEAR) or -2 (FAR).

SIZE	Format: `SIZE variable` Returns a count of the number of bytes allocated for the variable.
LENGTH	Format: `LENGTH variable` Returns a count of the number of units (bytes or words) allocated for the variable.
Attribute **PTR**	Format: `type PTR expression` Overrides the type (BYTE or WORD) or distance (NEAR or FAR) of a memory address operand. *type* is the new attribute and *expression* is the identifier whose attribute is to be overridden.

DS:
ES:
SS:
	Format: `seg-reg:addr-expr`
	              or
	              `seg-reg:label`
	              or
	              `seg-reg:variable`
	Overrides the segment attribute of a label, variable, or address expression.

SHORT	Format: `JMP SHORT label` Modifies the NEAR attribute of a JMP target label to indicate it is no farther than +127 or −128 bytes from the next instruction.

The assembler also has a MOD operator that returns the *remainder* of a divide operation. The statement

```
PI_REM EQU 31416 MOD 10000
```

defines a constant called PI_REM that has the value 1416.

Finally, operators SHL and SHR shift a numeric operand left or right. About the only time you need this capability is when you set up "masks" that you will apply to binary patterns in memory. For example, if you set up a mask with the statement

```
MASK EQU 110010B
```

the statement

```
MASK_LEFT_2 EQU MASK SHL 2
```

sets up a new constant with the value 11001000B. Similarly,

```
MASK_RIGHT_2 EQU MASK SHR 2
```

sets up a new constant with the value 1100B.

Logical Operators

Like SHL and SHR in the preceding section, the logical operators are used primarily to manipulate binary values. The logical operators manipulate individual bits, however, rather than an entire group of bits.

To draw an analogy, imagine a group of patients seated on a bench at a medical clinic. If the clinic operates in "shift" fashion, the nurse may order the first three patients to report to treatment rooms and ask the remaining patients to shift left. In doing this, the nurse essentially performs an *SHL 3* operation.

Conversely, if the clinic operates in "logical" fashion, the nurse may order just certain patients (perhaps only those with broken bones) to report to the treatment rooms and tell the remaining patients to stay where they are on the bench.

The logical operators AND, OR, and XOR combine two operands to produce a result; NOT requires just one operand. Table 2–8 shows how AND, OR, and XOR operate.

AND is primarily used to filter, mask, or strip out certain bits. To do this, AND sets the result bit to 1 for each bit position in which both operands contain a 1. For any other bit combination, AND clears the result bit to 0.

For example, the operation

```
00110100B AND 11010111B
```

Table 2–8. The AND, OR, and XOR combinations.

		Result		
Operand #1	Operand #2	AND	OR	XOR
0	0	0	0	0
0	1	0	1	1
1	0	0	1	1
1	1	1	1	0

produces the result 00010100B. As you can see, AND operates like a house with a double-lock door. If neither lock is engaged (1 = unlocked), you can enter the house, but if either or both locks are engaged (0 = locked), you are shut outside. Here, a "1" result means you can enter and a "0" result means you cannot enter.

OR sets the result bit to 1 for each position in which either or both operands contain a 1. Conversely, for bit positions where both operands contain 0, OR clears the result bit to 0. For example,

```
00110100B or 11010111B
```

produces the result 11110111B. To make another "door" analogy, OR operates like a house with two doors. If either or both doors are unlocked (1 = unlocked), you can enter the house, but if both doors are locked (0 = locked), you are shut outside.

XOR is a variation of OR wherein 1s in both operands produce a 0, rather than a 1, in the result. The name XOR is derived from "exclusive-OR" (because it excludes the 1-and-1 combination), to distinguish it from the "inclusive-OR" condition labeled OR.

NOT simply reverses the state of each bit in the operand. That is, it changes each 1 to 0 and each 0 to 1. For example,

```
NOT 01101001B
```

produces the result 10010110B.

The 8086 also has assembly language instructions named AND, OR, XOR, and NOT, which we discuss in Chapter 3. The basic difference is that the logical operators do their job when the program *assembles*, while the logical instructions do their job when the program *executes*.

Relational Operators

Relational operators compare two numeric values or memory addresses in the same segment, and produce a 0 result if the relationship is "false" or 0FFFFH if the relationship is "true."

For example, if CHOICE is a predefined constant, the statement

```
MOV AX,CHOICE LT 20
```

assembles as

```
MOV AX,0FFFFH
```

if CHOICE is less than 20, and as

```
MOV AX,0
```

if CHOICE is greater than or equal to 20.

Because the relational operators can produce only two values, 0 or 0FFFFH, they are rarely used alone. Instead, they are usually combined with other operators to form a decision-making expression. For instance, suppose AX is to receive the value 5 if CHOICE is less than 20 and 6 otherwise. A statement that performs this task is

```
MOV AX,((CHOICE LT 20) AND 5) OR ((CHOICE GE 20)
    AND 6)
```

Here, if CHOICE is less than 20, (CHOICE LT 20) is "true" and (CHOICE GE 20) is "false." Hence, the intermediate form of the statement is

```
MOV AX,(0FFFFH AND 5) OR (0 AND 6)
```

which the assembler evaluates as

```
MOV AX,5
```

Conversely, if CHOICE is greater than or equal to 20, (CHOICE LT 20) is "false" and (CHOICE GE 20) is "true." In this case, the intermediate form of the statement is

```
MOV AX,(0 AND 5) or (0FFFFH AND 6)
```

which the assembler evaluates as

```
MOV AX,6
```

Value-Returning Operators

This group contains operators that provide information about variables and labels in your program.

The *SEG* and *OFFSET* operators return the segment and offset values of a variable or label. For example, the statements

```
MOV AX,SEG TABLE
MOV BX,OFFSET TABLE
```

load the segment and offset values of TABLE into AX and BX, respectively. (Since segment and offset are both 16-bit values, they can only be loaded into 16-bit registers.)

TYPE returns a numeric value to indicate the type attribute of a variable or the distance attribute of a label. When applied to a variable, TYPE returns 1 for a BYTE variable and 2 for a WORD variable. When applied to a label, TYPE returns −1 for a NEAR label and −2 for a FAR label.

The *LENGTH* and *SIZE* operators are meaningful only with variables you define with DUP. LENGTH returns the number of bytes or words allocated for the variable. For example, the sequence.

```
TABLE DW   100 DUP(1)
      MOV CX,LENGTH TABLE ;Get number of words
                         ;   in TABLE
```

loads 100 into CX. If you use LENGTH with any other kind of variable, it returns the value 1.

SIZE returns the byte count of a variable. (That is, SIZE returns the product of LENGTH times TYPE.) Using the variable TABLE we just defined, the statement

```
MOV CX,SIZE TABLE ;Get no. of bytes in TABLE
```

loads 200 into CS.

Attribute Operators

Attribute operators let you specify a new attribute for an operand, and thereby override its current attribute.

The pointer (PTR) operator overrides the type (BYTE or WORD) or distance (NEAR or FAR) attribute of an operand. For instance, PTR can reference bytes in a table of words. As an example, if you define a table as

```
WORD_TABLE DW 100 DUP(?)
```

the statement

```
FIRST_BYTE EQU BYTE PTR WORD_TABLE
```

assigns the name FIRST_BYTE to the location of the first byte in WORD_____

TABLE. After that, you can name any other byte as easily as this:

```
FIFTH_BYTE EQU FIRST_BYTE+4
```

As we just mentioned, PTR can also change the distance attribute of a label. For example, if we have this instruction in a program:

```
START: MOV CX,100
```

the colon suffix on the label gives START a NEAR distance attribute, which allows jump instructions in the same segment to reference the MOV instruction like this:

```
JMP START
```

To jump to START from a different segment, you must rename START with a FAR attribute. This kind of sequence will do the job:

```
FAR_START EQU FAR PTR START
          JMP FAR_START
```

The *segment override* operator (DS:, ES:, or SS:) overrides the segment attribute of a label, variable, or address expression. As we mentioned in Chapter 1, when calculating a memory address, the 8086 automatically assumes SS is the segment register if the operand employs SP or BP to hold the offset. Similarly, it assumes DS is the segment register if the operand employs BX, SI, or DI to hold the offset.

The segment override operator lets you specify an alternate segment register. For example, the override

```
MOV AX,ES:[BP]
```

directs the 8086 to use ES, rather than SS, to calculate the memory address.

The *SHORT* operator tells the assembler that a JMP target is within +127 or −128 bytes of the next instruction. With this information, the assembler makes JMP a 2-byte, rather than 3-byte, instruction, which saves memory. Here is an example:

```
          JMP SHORT THERE
          . .
          . .
THERE:
```

2.8 Sample Program

Since we haven't discussed the details of the 8086's assembly language instructions (that's coming in Chapter 3), you cannot yet write programs that add or subtract numbers, manipulate the registers, or perform the many other tasks you eventually want your computer to do. Still, you *do* have enough information to write a program that moves data around with MOV instructions and sets up the necessary segments with assembler directives.

In this section we will look at a program that copies one 4-byte data table in memory into another. To make it more interesting, we will store the data in the "destination" table in the reverse order it is stored in the "source" table.

The details of this program are unimportant, however. The important point is that you will learn what a "real" program should look like. You should also use your own computer to enter the program, then assemble it with your assembler and run it using your disk operating system (DOS). With those steps aside, you can proceed with confidence through the more complex material in the rest of the book.

Figure 2–1 lists the instructions for our table-copying program. Note that it has a stack segment, a data segment, and a code segment.

The *stack segment* (MY_STACK) will hold a return address that puts you back in DOS when the program has finished executing. (DOS is responsible for putting this address on the stack.) We arbitrarily make the stack 10 words long here, but you need only enough memory to hold all of the information that will be "pushed" on the stack. (We discuss stacks in detail later in the book.)

The *data segment* (MY_DATA) holds the data table we want to copy (SOURCE) and a reservation for 4 bytes where we will copy the table to (DEST).

The *code segment* holds the program itself. To begin, we tell the assembler (with ASSUME) which segment register applies to our three segments. Then we put the proper segment numbers in DS and SS and make the stack pointer (SP) point to the top of the stack, a location labeled STK_TOP.

```
; This program moves a 4-byte table (SOURCE)
; into another table (DEST) in the data segment.
; Registers used:  AX
            NAME       EXAMPLE
;
; Here is the stack segment.
MY_STACK SEGMENT   PARA STACK 'STACK'
         DW        10 DUP(?)
STK_TOP  LABEL     WORD
MY_STACK ENDS
;
; Here is the data segment.
MY_DATA  SEGMENT   PARA 'DATA'
SOURCE   DB        10,20,30,40          ;Source table
```

```
DEST        DB          4 DUP(?)                ;Destination
                                                ; table
MY_DATA     ENDS
;
; Here is the code segment (program).
MY_CODE     SEGMENT     PARA 'CODE'
MY_PROG     PROC        FAR
            ASSUME      CS:MY_CODE,DS:MY_DATA,SS:MY_STACK
;
; Initialize data segment and stack segment
; registers and set stack pointer to top of
; stack.
            MOV         AX,MY_DATA
            MOV         DS,AX
            MOV         AX,MY_STACK
            MOV         SS,AX
            MOV         SP,OFFSET STK_TOP
;
; Fill DEST with zeros.
            MOV         DEST,0                  ;First byte
            MOV         DEST+1,0                ;Second byte
            MOV         DEST+2,0                ;Third byte
            MOV         DEST+3,0                ;Fourth byte
;
; Copy SOURCE table into DEST table, in reverse
; order.
            MOV         AL,SOURCE               ;Copy first
                                                ; byte
            MOV         DEST+3,AL
            MOV         AL,SOURCE+1             ;Copy second
                                                ; byte
            MOV         DEST+2,AL
            MOV         AL,SOURCE+2             ;Copy third
                                                ; byte
            MOV         DEST+1,AL
            MOV         AL,SOURCE+3             ;Copy fourth
                                                ; byte
            MOV         DEST,AL
            RET                                 ;Return to
                                                ; caller
MY_PROG     ENDP
MY_CODE     ENDS
            END         MY_PROG
```

Figure 2–1. Table-copying program.

With all of this "housekeeping" out of the way, we fill the destination table (DEST) with zeros. This step is necessary so that each time you run the program and check the final contents of DEST, you know you are looking at the program's effect on DEST, not just the results of the previous run. Finally, we copy the table data 1 byte at a time, then return to DOS.

The instructions in the code segment are a single procedure enclosed by the statements *MY PROG PROC FAR* and *MY PROG ENDP*. Because the procedure has a FAR attribute, the final RET instruction returns the 8086 to DOS, which is in a different segment in memory The FAR attribute sets up RET to remove two addresses from the stack: an offset and a segment number. *For these same reasons, most of the programs you write should be defined as procedures.*

After you have entered this program into your computer and saved it on disk, assemble it using your assembler, then run it using either DOS or a debug program. The debug program is preferable because you can run the program one instruction at a time (that is, "single-step") and examine the registers and memory locations as you go.

Exercises (answers on page 205)

1. How many *bytes* does the following sequence allocate in memory?

```
VAR1  DB  ?
VAR2  DW  4 DUP(?),20
VAR3  DB  10 DUP(?)
```

2. What value does the assembler put into VAR1 in Exercise 1?
3. Tell what is wrong with this sequence:

```
CONST DB   ?
      MOV CONST,256
```

4. Which two directives must appear in every procedure?
5. What is the difference between a NEAR procedure and a FAR procedure?
6. Which assembler directive must appear in every source program?

3

The 8086/8088 Instruction Set

3.1 About This Chapter

In Chapter 2 you began working with the "foundation" of assembly language—the instructions that control the microprocessor. This chapter provides a detailed description of the 8086's (and 8088's) instruction set and operand addressing modes.

Many books cover the instructions individually, discussing them one by one, in alphabetical order. Although that approach has definite merit in a technical reference manual, it tends to leave you bored and bewildered after the fifth or sixth instruction.

In this book, we group instructions by function, so similar instructions are described together. That is, we group add instructions with subtract instructions, shift instructions with rotate instructions, and so on. This approach is intended to help you *understand* the instruction set, and how individual instructions "fit together," so you don't learn them as just a lot of disjointed entities.

Later, after running a few programs, you will need to refer to this chapter only occasionally, to look up the details of specific instructions. Once you feel comfortable with the instruction set, you can resolve most questions by referring to Appendix D, where the instructions are summarized alphabetically. Appendix C is also useful; it tells you how long each instruction takes to execute.

3.2 Addressing Modes

The 8086 provides a variety of ways to access the operands your programs are to operate on. Operands can be contained in registers, within the instruction itself, or in memory or an I/O port. Some of the manufacturers' marketing literature claims that the 8086 has 24 operand addressing modes—perhaps justifiably, if you consider all the possible operand combinations. In this book, however, we divide the addressing modes into seven groups:

1. Register addressing
2. Immediate addressing
3. Direct addressing
4. Register indirect addressing
5. Base relative addressing
6. Direct indexed addressing
7. Base indexed addressing

The microprocessor determines *which* of the seven addressing modes to use by examining the contents of a "mode field" in the instruction. The bits in the mode field are encoded by the assembler, based on how the operand(s) appear in your source program. For instance, if you write

```
MOV AX,BX
```

the assembler encodes both operands (*AX* and *BX*) for the register addressing mode. If, however, you put brackets around the source operand, and write the instruction as

```
MOV AX,[BX]
```

the assembler encodes the source operand (BX) for the register *indirect* addressing mode.

Table 3–1 shows the assembler format, and which segment register is used to calculate the physical address, for the 8086's seven operand addressing modes. Note that all modes assume you are accessing the data segement (DS is the segment register) except those that involve BP, in which case the stack segment is assumed (SS is the segment register).

> *Important*: The 8086's string instructions, which are described in Section 3.8, assume that DI references a location in the extra segment, rather than the data segment, and use ES as the segment register. All other instructions follow the assignments in Table 3–1.

Of the seven addressing modes, the 8086 processes register and immediate operands fastest, because its Execution Unit (EU) can fetch them from registers (for register addressing) or from the instruction queue (for immediate addressing). The five other modes take longer to process because the Bus Interface Unit (BIU) must compute a memory address, then fetch the operand and pass it to the EU.

Each addressing mode description in this section includes an example of the mode's usage. In most cases, we use the 8086's move instruction to demonstrate the mode.

Table 3–1. 8086 addressing modes.

Addressing Mode	Operand Format	Segment Register
Register	`reg`	None
Immediate	`data`	None
Direct	`disp`	DS
	`label`	DS
Register indirect	`[BX]`	DS
	`[BP]`	SS
	`[DI]`	DS
	`[SI]`	DS
Base relative	`[BX]+disp`	DS
	`[BP]+disp`	SS
Direct indexed	`[DI]+disp`	DS
	`[SI]+disp`	DS
Base indexed	`[BX][SI]+disp`	DS
	`[BX][DI]+disp`	DS
	`[BP][SI]+disp`	SS
	`[BP][DI]+disp`	SS

Notes: 1. *disp* is optional for base indexed addressing.
2. *reg* can be any 8- or 16-bit register, except IP.
3. *data* can be an 8- or 16-bit constant value.
4. *disp* can be an 8- or 16-bit signed displacement value.

Register and Immediate Addressing

In *register addressing*, the 8086 fetches an operand from (or loads it into) a register. For example, the instruction

```
MOV AX,CX
```

copies the 16-bit contents of the count register (CX) into the accumulator register (AX). The contents of CX are unaffected. In this example, the 8086 uses register addressing to fetch the source operand from CX and to load it into the destination register, AX.

Immediate addressing lets you specify an 8- or 16-bit constant value as a source operand. This constant is contained in the instruction (where it was put by the assembler), rather than in a register or a memory location. For example,

```
MOV CX,500
```

loads the value 500 into the CX register and

```
MOV CL,-30
```

loads −30 into the CL register.

The immediate operand may also be a symbol that was defined by an EQU directive, so this kind of form is valid:

```
K  EQU  1024
    ..
    ..
  MOV  CX,K
```

To avoid problems, remember that 8-bit signed numbers are limited to values between 127 (7FH) and −128 (80H), and that 16-bit signed numbers are limited to values between 32767 (7FFFH) and −32768 (8000H). For unsigned numbers, the maximum 8- and 16-bit values are 255 (0FFH) and 65535 (0FFFFH), respectively.

Immediate Values Are Sign-Extended

Immediate values are always sign-extended in the destination. This means the most-significant bit of the source value is replicated to fill the 8 or 16 bits of the destination operand.

For instance, the source operand for our first example, decimal 500, can be represented by the 10-bit binary pattern 0111110100. When the assembler realizes that you are loading this value into a 16-bit register (CX), it extends the pattern to 16 bits by preceding it with six copies of the "sign" bit value (0). Therefore, CX will end up containing the binary pattern *0000000111110100*.

In the second example, the 8088 loads the 8-bit binary pattern for −30 (11100010) into CL.

Memory Addressing Modes

As we mentioned in Chapter 1, accessing memory involves a joint effort by the 8086's Execution Unit (EU) and Bus Interface Unit (BIU). When the EU needs to read or write a memory operand, it must pass an offset value to the BIU. The BIU adds this offset to the contents of a segment register (with four 0s appended) to produce a 20-bit physical address, then uses that address to access the operand.

The Effective Address

The offset that the Execution Unit calculates for a memory operand is called the operand's *effective address* (EA). The EA represents the operand's distance in bytes from the beginning of the segment where it resides. Being a 16-bit unsigned value, the EA can reference operands that lie up to 65,535 bytes beyond the first location of the segment.

The amount of time the Execution Unit takes to calculate the EA is one of the prime factors in determining how long an instruction takes to execute. Depending on which addressing mode is used, deriving the EA may involve nothing more than fetching a displacement from within the instruction. Then again, it may require some lengthy calculation, such as adding a displacement, a base register, and an index register. Even if the execution time is not critical in the application programs you write, it is worthwhile to appreciate these time factors as you read the addressing mode descriptions that follow.

Direct Addressing

With direct addressing, the EA is contained in the instruction, just as the immediate data value is contained in an immediate instruction. The 8086 adds the EA to the (shifted) contents of the Data Segment (DS) register to produce the operand's 20-bit physical address.

The direct addressing operand is generally a label, rather than a displacement value. For example, the instruction

```
MOV AX,TABLE
```

loads the contents of data memory location TABLE into the AX register. Figure 3–1 shows how this instruction works.

Incidentally, note that the 8086 stores the data in memory in the reverse order you would expect to find it: with the high-order byte *following* (rather than preceding) the low-order byte. To keep this straight, just remember that *the high (most-significant) part of the data is in the highest memory address.*

Register Indirect Addressing

With register indirect addressing, the effective address of the operand is contained in base register BX, base pointer BP, or an index register (SI or DI). You must enclose register indirect operands in square brackets

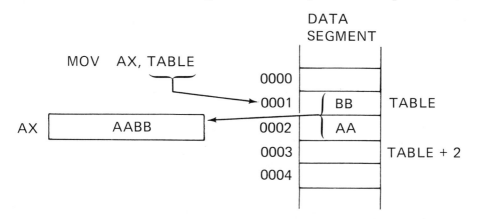

Figure 3–1. Direct addressing.

to differentiate them from register operands. For example, the instruction

```
MOV AX,[BX]
```

loads the contents of the memory location addressed by BX into the AX register. Figure 3–2 illustrates this example.

How do you put an offset address into BX? One way is by applying the OFFSET operator to the memory address. For instance, to load the word at location *TABLE* into AX, you could use the sequence

```
MOV BX,OFFSET TABLE
MOV AX,[BX]
```

These two instructions do the same job as the single instruction

```
MOV AX,TABLE
```

except that they destroy the previous contents of BX. If you plan to access just one memory location (the contents of TABLE here), this single-instruction approach makes more sense. If, however, you plan to access *several* locations, starting at that base address, having the effective address in a register is the better approach. Why? Because you can manipulate the contents of the register without fetching a new address each time.

Base Relative Addressing

With base relative addressing, the effective address is the sum of a displacement value plus the contents of the BX or BP register.

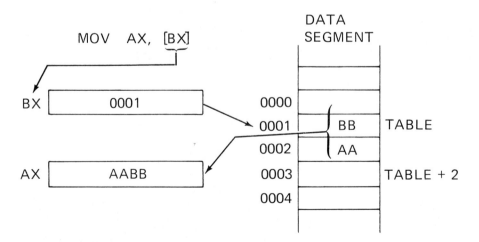

Figure 3–2. Register indirect addressing.

The BX form gives you a convenient way to access data structures located at different places in memory. To do this, you put the base address of the structure into the base register and reference elements of the structure by their displacement from the base. After that, you can access different records in the structure by simply changing the base register.

For example, suppose you have read some personnel records into memory from disk. Each record contains an employee's identification number, department number, division number, age, pay rate, and so on. If the division number is stored in the fifth and sixth bytes of the record, and the starting address of the record is in BX, the instruction

```
MOV AX,[BX]+4
```

loads the employee's division number into AX. (The displacement is 4, rather than 5, because the first byte is Byte 0.) Figure 3–3 illustrates this example.

Just as we used BX to access a location in the data segment, we can use BP to access stack data. The instruction

```
MOV AX,[BP]+4
```

loads the contents of the fourth location after the BP address into AX.

ASM-86 lets you specify the base relative operand in three different ways. The following are equivalent instructions:

```
MOV AX,[BP]+4    ;This is the standard form, but
MOV AX,4[BP]     ; you may put the displacement
MOV AX,[BP+4]    ; first or within the brackets
```

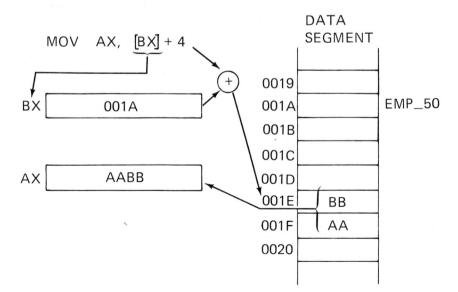

Figure 3–3. Base relative addressing.

Direct Indexed Addressing

With direct indexed addressing, the effective address is the sum of a displacement and an index register, either DI or SI. You often use this type of addressing to access elements in a table. There, the displacement points to the beginning of the table and the index register points to an element in the table.

For example, if we have a byte table called B_TABLE, the instruction sequence

```
MOV DI,2
MOV AL,B_TABLE[DI]
```

loads the table's third element (a byte value) into the AL register.

In a word table, the elements lie 2 bytes apart, so you *double the element number* to get its index value. With a word table called TABLE, the instruction sequence

```
MOV DI,4
MOV AX,TABLE[DI]
```

loads the table's third element (a word value) into the AX register. Figure 3–4 illustrates this example.

Base Indexed Addressing

With base indexed addressing, the EA is the sum of three components: a base register, an index register, and a displacement. (The displacement is optional and may be omitted.)

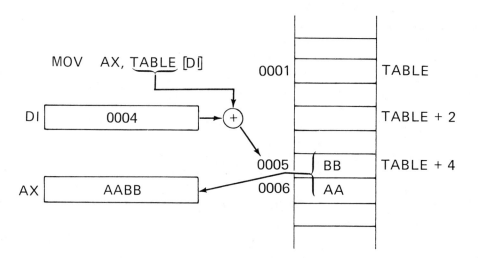

Figure 3–4. Direct indexed addressing.

Because it offers two separate offsets, base indexed addressing is useful for accessing two-dimensional arrays. For such applications, a base register holds the starting address of the array, and the displacement and index register provide row and column offsets.

For example, suppose your computer monitors six pressure valves in a chemical processing plant. This system reads the valve settings every half-hour and records them in memory. In one week, these readings will form an array that has 336 blocks (48 readings per day for seven days) of six elements each, a total of 2,016 data values.

If the starting address of the array is in BX, the block displacement (reading number times 12) is in DI, and the valve number displacement is defined by the variable VALVE, you can use the instruction

```
MOV AX,VALVE[BX][DI]
```

to load any selected pressure valve reading into AX. In Figure 3–5, this instruction extracts the third reading (Reading 2) of Valve 4 from an array that has a data segment offset of 100H.

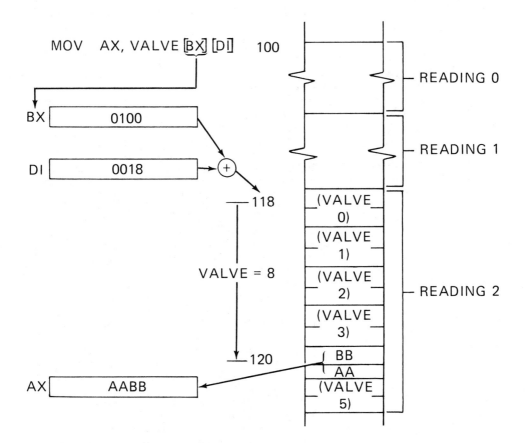

Figure 3–5. Extracting a data value from a two-dimensional array.

Here are some other legal formats for base indexed addressing operands:

```
MOV AX,[BX+2+DI]     ;The operands can be put in
MOV AX,[DI+BX+2]     ; brackets in any order
MOV AX,[BX+2][DI]    ; and the displacement can be
MOV AX,[BX][DI+2]    ; paired with either register
```

3.3 Instruction Types

As we mentioned earlier, the 8086 has 92 basic instruction types. Table 3–2 shows their assembler mnemonics and tells you what each mnemonic stands for. Note that some instructions have several valid mnemonics.

We can divide the instruction set into seven functional groups:

1. *Data transfer instructions* move information between registers and memory locations or I/O ports.
2. *Arithmetic instructions* perform arithmetic operations on binary or binary-coded decimal (BCD) numbers.
3. *Bit manipulation instructions* perform shift, rotate, and logical operations on memory locations and registers.
4. *Control transfer instructions* perform jumps, calls to procedures, and returns from procedures to control the sequence in which a program executes.
5. *String instructions* move, compare, and scan strings of information.
6. *Interrupt instructions* interrupt the microprocessor to make sure it can service some specific condition.
7. *Processor control instructions* set and clear status flags, and change the microprocessor's execution state.

Table 3–2. The 8086/8088 instruction set.

Mnemonic	*Description*
AAA	ASCII Adjust for Addition
AAD	ASCII Adjust for Division
AAM	ASCII Adjust for Multiplication
AAS	ASCII Adjust for Subtraction
ADC	Add with Carry
ADD	Add (without Carry)
AND	Logical AND
CALL	Call a Procedure
CBW	Convert Byte to Word
CLC	Clear Carry Flag
CLD	Clear Direction Flag
CLI	Clear Interrupt Flag
CMC	Complement Carry Flag
CMP	Compare Destination to Source
CMPS, CMPSB, or **CMPSW**	Compare Byte or Word Strings

Table 3–2. The 8086/8088 instruction set (continued).

Mnemonic	Description
CWD	Convert Word to Doubleword
DAA	Decimal Adjust for Addition
DAS	Decimal Adjust for Subtraction
DEC	Decrement Destination by One
DIV	Divide, Unsigned
ESC	Escape
HLT	Halt the Processor
INDIV	Integer Divide, Signed
IMUL	Integer Multiply, Signed
IN	Input Byte or Word
INC	Increment Destination by One
INT	Interrupt
INTO	Interrupt If Overflow
IRET	Interrupt Return
JA or JNBE	Jump If Above/If Not Below Nor Equal
JAE, JNB, or JNC	Jump If Above or Equal/If Not Below/If No Carry
JB, JNAE, or JC	Jump If Below/If Not Above Nor Equal/If Carry
JBE or JNA	Jump If Below or Equal/If Not Above
JCXZ	Jump If CX Is Zero
JE or JZ	Jump If Equal/If Zero
JG or JNLE	Jump If Greater/If Not Less Nor Equal
JGE or JNL	Jump If Greater or Equal/If Not Less
JL or JNGE	Jump If Less/If Not Greater Nor Equal
JLE or JNG	Jump If Less or Equal/If Not Greater
JMP	Jump Unconditionally
JNE or JNZ	Jump If Not Equal/If Not Zero
JNO	Jump If No Overflow
JNP or JPO	Jump If No Parity/If Parity Odd
JNS	Jump If No Sign (If Positive)
JO	Jump on Overflow
JP or JPE	Jump on Parity/If Parity Even
JS	Jump on Sign
LAHF	Load AH from Flags
LDS	Load Pointer Using DS
LEA	Load Effective Address
LES	Load Pointer Using ES
LOCK	Lock the Bus
LODS, LODSB, or LODSW	Load Byte or Word String
LOOP	Loop until Count Complete
LOOPE or LOOPZ	Loop While Equal/While Zero
LOOPNE or LOOPNZ	Loop While Not Equal/While Not Zero
MOV	Move

Table 3–2. The 8086/8088 instruction set (continued).

Mnemonic	Description
MOVS, MOVSB, or MOVSW	Move Byte or Word String
MUL	Multiply, Unsigned
NEG	Negate (Form Twos-Complement)
NOP	No Operation
NOT	Logical NOT
OR	Logical Inclusive-OR
OUT	Output Byte or Word
POP	Pop Word off Stack to Destination
POPF	Pop Flags off Stack
PUSH	Push Word onto Stack
PUSHF	Push Flags onto Stack
RCL	Rotate Left through Carry
RCR	Rotate Right through Carry
REP, REPE, or REPZ	Repeat String Operation/While Equal/While Zero
REPNE or REPNZ	Repeat String Operation While Not Equal/While Not Zero
RET	Return from Procedure
ROL	Rotate Left
ROR	Rotate Right
SAHF	Store AH into Flags
SAL or SHL	Shift Arithmetic Left/Logical Left
SAR	Shift Arithmetic Right
SBB	Subtract with Borrow
SCAS, SCASB, or SCASW	Scan Byte or Word String
SHR	Shift Logical Right
STC	Set Carry Flag
STD	Set Direction Flag
STI	Set Interrupt Enable Flag
STOS, STOSB, or STOSW	Store Byte or Word String
SUB	Subtract (without Borrow)
TEST	Test (Logically Compare Two Operands)
WAIT	Wait
XCHG	Exchange Two Operands
XLAT	Translate
XOR	Logical Exclusive-OR

In the following sections we will describe the 8086 instruction set by groups, in the order just presented. Let us begin with the data transfer group, which includes the ubiquitous MOV instruction.

3.4 Data Transfer Instructions

Data transfer instructions move data and addresses between registers and memory locations or I/O ports. Table 3–3 summarizes these instructions and groups them into four categories: general-purpose, input/output, address transfer, and flag transfer.

General-Purpose Instructions

Move (MOV)

The fundamental general-purpose instruction is *move (MOV)*, which can transfer byte or word data between a register and a memory location, or between two registers. It can also transfer an immediate data value into a register or memory location.

The move instruction has the general form

```
MOV destination,source
```

Table 3–3. Data transfer instructions.

			Flags								
Mnemonic		Assembler Format	OF	DF	IF	TF	SF	ZF	AF	PF	CF
GENERAL PURPOSE											
MOV	MOV	destination, source	—	—	—	—	—	—	—	—	—
PUSH	PUSH	source	—	—	—	—	—	—	—	—	—
POP	POP	destination	—	—	—	—	—	—	—	—	—
XCHG	XCHG	destination,source	—	—	—	—	—	—	—	—	—
XLAT	XLAT	source-table	—	—	—	—	—	—	—	—	—
INPUT/OUTPUT											
IN	IN	accumulator,port	—	—	—	—	—	—	—	—	—
OUT	OUT	port,accumulator	—	—	—	—	—	—	—	—	—
ADDRESS TRANSFER											
LEA	LEA	reg16,mem16	—	—	—	—	—	—	—	—	—
LDS	LDS	reg16,mem32	—	—	—	—	—	—	—	—	—
LES	LES	reg16,mem32	—	—	—	—	—	—	—	—	—
FLAG TRANSFER											
LAHF	LAHF		—	—	—	—	—	—	—	—	—
SAHF	SAHF		—	—	—	—	*	*	*	*	*
PUSHF	PUSHF		—	—	—	—	—	—	—	—	—
POPF	POPF		*	*	*	*	*	*	*	*	*

Note: * means changed and — means unchanged.

Most operand combinations are legal. Here are some examples:

```
MOV   AX,TABLE      ;Move from memory into a
MOV   TABLE,AX      ; register or vice versa
MOV   ES:[BX],AX    ;A segment override may be
                    ; included
MOV   DS,AX         ;Move between 16-bit registers
MOV   BL,AL         ; or 8-bit registers
MOV   CL,-30        ;Move a constant into a
MOV   DEST,25H      ; register or into memory
```

The move instruction *excludes* these combinations:

1. You cannot move data between two memory locations directly. To do this, move the source data into a general-purpose register, then move *that* register into the destination. For example, if POUNDS and WEIGHT are variables in memory, give them the same value with:

   ```
   MOV AX,POUNDS
   MOV WEIGHT,AX
   ```

2. You cannot load an immediate value into a segment register. As with Rule 1, load it via a general-purpose register. For example, the following loads the segment number of a data segment (DATA_SEG here) into DS:

   ```
   MOV AX,DATA_SEG
   MOV DS,AX
   ```

   These kinds of instructions follow the ASSUME statement in a code segment. They tell the assembler where the data segment is located.

3. You cannot move the contents of one segment register into another directly. Make the move via a general-purpose register. For example, to make DS point to the same segment as ES, use

   ```
   MOV AX,ES
   MOV DS,AX
   ```

   You can also use PUSH and POP instructions to perform this operation, as you will see in the next section.
4. You cannot use the CS register as the destination of a move instruction.

Push (PUSH) and Pop (POP)

We mentioned earlier that the stack holds return addresses while a procedure is being executed. The call (CALL instruction) pushes an address onto the stack and a return (RET) instruction retrieves it at the end of the procedure. This is one of the ways the 8086 uses the stack *automatically*, without your telling it is doing so.

The stack is also a convenient place, however, to temporarily deposit data—register and memory operands—from your program. For instance, you might want to save the contents of the AX register while you put AX to some other use. Two instructions that let you access the stack are *Push Word onto Stack (PUSH)* and *Pop Word off Stack (POP)*.

PUSH puts a word-sized register or memory operand on the top of the stack. Conversely, POP retrieves a word from the top of the stack and puts it into memory or a register.

The PUSH and POP instructions have these general formats:

```
PUSH  source
POP   destination
```

In both cases, the operand can be a 16-bit register or a word-sized memory location. Here are some examples:

```
PUSH  SI              ;You can save a general-
                      ; purpose register
PUSH  DS              ; or a segment register,
PUSH  CS              ; including CS
PUSH  COUNTER         ;You can also save the
                      ; contents of
PUSH  TABLE[BX][DI]   ; a memory location
```

Being complementary, PUSH and POP instructions are generally used in pairs. That is, for each PUSH in a program there must be a POP. For example, to save the contents of AX on the stack and later restore them, your program would have this form:

```
PUSH  AX   ;Save AX on top of the stack
..             (Other operations are being
..              performed with AX here.)
POP   AX   ;Retrieve AX from top of the stack
```

What do we mean by the "top" of the stack? We mean the location in the stack segment the stack pointer (SP) is pointing to. The SP always points to the word that was last pushed onto the stack. Since the stack "builds" downward in memory (at ever-decreasing addresses), the first word pushed onto the stack is stored at the highest stack address, the next word pushed is stored 2 bytes lower, and so on.

PUSH substracts 2 from the stack pointer, then transfers the source operand (a word) onto the stack. Conversely, POP transfers the word addressed by SP to the destination operand, then adds 2 to the SP.

To illustrate these points, Figure 3–6 shows the stack and the stack pointer before and after a PUSH, and after a POP. After the PUSH (Figure 3–6B), the stack pointer has moved 2 bytes lower in memory and those previously-unused bytes now hold the contents of AX. After the POP (Figure 3–6C), the SP has resumed its original position. Although AX is still in memory, it is not "on the stack."

You can also save more than one word value on a stack, by performing a series of pushes. In doing so, however, remember that because each

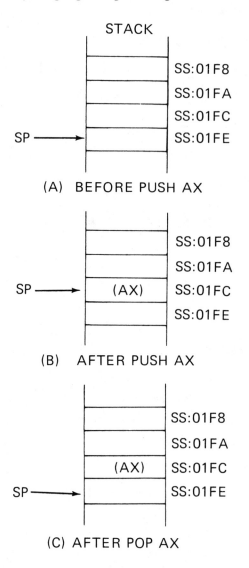

Figure 3–6. How a PUSH and a POP
affect the stack.

PUSH puts its data on top of the stack, *you must POP words off the stack in the reverse order you PUSHed them onto the stack.* Here is a sequence that pushes the contents of four registers onto the stack, and later restores them:

```
PUSH  AX    ;Save AX,
PUSH  ES    ; ES,
PUSH  DI    ; DI,
PUSH  SI    ; and SI
 . .

 . .
POP   SI    ;Restore SI,
POP   DI    ; DI,
```

```
POP    ES  ; ES,
POP    AX  ; and AX
```

Finally, PUSH and POP are also convenient for moving the contents of one segment register into another. For example, you could copy ES into DS as follows:

```
PUSH ES
POP  DS
```

The advantage of this approach is that it doesn't require you to use a general-purpose register for intermediate storage (see the preceding section); the disadvantage is that the PUSH-POP combination takes 26 clock cycles to execute, as opposed to 4 cycles with a pair of MOV instructions.

There are also special instructions that push and pop the contents of the flags register. We'll look at them in the *Flags Transfer* portion of this section.

Exchange (XCHG)

The exchange (XCHG) instruction exchanges the byte or word source operand with the destination operand. With XCHG you can exchange the contents of two registers, or exchange the contents of a register and a memory location. Segment registers may not be used as operands with XCHG.

Some examples are:

```
XCHG   AX,BX          ;Exchange two word registers
XCHG   AL,BH          ; or two byte registers
XCHG   WORD_LOC,DX    ;Exchange a memory location
XCHG   DL,BYTE_LOC    ; and a register
```

Translate (XLAT)

The translate (XLAT) instruction looks up a value in a byte table and loads it into AL. The table may be up to 256 bytes long.

The general format of the XLAT instruction is

```
XLAT source-table
```

where *source-table* is the name of the look-up table. Before you execute XLAT, you must load the table's starting address into BX and the index value of the byte you want to access into AL.

This sequence looks up the tenth byte in the table S_TAB:

```
MOV    AL,10           ;Load index value into AL
MOV    BX,OFFSET S_TAB ;Load offset address into
                       ; BX
XLAT S_TAB             ;Fetch table value into
                       AL
```

XLAT is convenient for making conversions that take a lot of time to calculate, such as finding the ASCII or EBCDIC code for a hexadecimal digit.

Input/Output Instructions

You use the input/output instructions to communicate with peripheral devices in the system. They have the general formats

```
IN   accumulator,port
OUT port,accumulator
```

where *accumulator* is AL for byte transfers and AX for word transfers. Generally, *port* is a decimal value between 0 and 255, in which case it references one of 256 devices in the system.

You may also use the DX register as the *port* operand, giving you access to 64K different ports. Using DX lets you change the port number easily, perhaps to send the same data to several different ports.

Here are a few examples of the IN and OUT instructions:

```
IN    AL,200        ;Input a byte from Port 200
IN    AL,PORT_VAL   ;Here the port is named by a
                    ; constant
OUT   30H,AX        ;Output a word to Port 30H
OUT   DX,AX         ;Output to the port specified
                     by DX
```

Address Transfer Instructions

Address transfer instructions transfer the *addresses* of variables rather than the *contents* of variables.

Load Effective Address (LEA)

LEA transfers the offset address of a memory operand into any 16-bit general, pointer, or index register. It has this general format:

```
LEA reg16,mem16
```

where *mem16* must have a type attribute of WORD.

Unlike MOV with an OFFSET operator, the memory operand for LEA can be subscripted, which gives you a lot more addressing flexibility. For example, if the DI register contains 5, the instruction

```
LEA BX,TABLE[DI]
```

loads the offset address of TABLE + 5 into BX.

We will discuss LEA instructions extensively in Section 3.8, where we perform operations on strings.

Load Pointer Using DS (LDS)

The LDS instruction fetches a 32-bit doubleword from memory, and loads the high-order 16 bits into a specified word register and the low-order 16 bits into DS. The general format is

```
LDS reg16,mem32
```

where *reg16* is any 16-bit general register and *mem32* is a memory location with a DOUBLEWORD type attribute.

Generally, the *mem32* operand is defined with the Define Doubleword (DD) data definition directive we discussed in Section 2.5. Using the example in that section,

```
HERE_FAR DD HERE
```

we can get the offset address and segment number of HERE into BX and DS, respectively, with the instruction

```
LDS BX,HERE_FAR
```

As you can see, LDS is a one-instruction replacement for a sequence of this kind:

```
MOV  BX,OFFSET HERE
MOV  AX,SEG HERE
MOV  DS,AX
```

Moreover, LDS eliminates the need for a third 16-bit register (AX, here).

Load Pointer Using ES (LES)

The LES instruction is identical to the LDS instruction, except LES transfers the segment word of the pointer into ES instead of DS.

Flag Transfer Instructions

Load AH from Flags (LAHF) and Store AH into Flags (SAHF)

The LAHF instructions copies the 8080/8085 flags in the flags register into AH. It copies CF, PF, AF, ZF, and SF into the corresponding bits of AH (0, 2, 4, 6, and 7, respectively).

The SAHF instruction performs the reverse operation. It loads the 5 bits of AH we just mentioned into the flags register.

LAHF does not affect any flags but, of course, SAHF affects the five 8080/8085 flags. Both instructions are provided for 8080/8085 compatibility.

Push Flags onto Stack (PUSHF) and Pop Flags off Stack (POPF)

These instructions transfer all 16 bits of the flags register (not just the 8080/8085 flags) to and from the stack. They are essentially the same as the PUSH and POP instructions, except PUSHF and POPF require no operands—they reference the flags register implicitly.

Like PUSH and POP, PUSHF and POPF are always *paired* in a program. That is, every PUSHF must have a corresponding POPF later in the program, like this:

```
PUSHF           ;Save flags on stacks
 . .            (Other flag-altering instructions are
 . .              executed here)
POPF            ;Restore flags from stack
```

Note that with PUSH, PUSHF, POP, and POPF, you can save any registers you choose (or *all* registers, if you like) while a procedure is being executed or an interrupt is being serviced. For instance, suppose you have some valuable data in AX, DI, and SI, and need to call a procedure named CLOBBER (because it clobbers your registers) that uses these registers. Suppose, also, you have just performed an arithmetic operation and need to have the flags intact after the procedure. This sequence should do the job for you:

```
PUSH    AX          ;Save the three registers
PUSH    DI
PUSH    SI
PUSHF               ; and the flags
CALL    CLOBBER     ;Call the procedure
POPF                ;Upon return, restore the flags
POP     SI          ; and the three registers
POP     DI
POP     AX
```

Better yet, you should put the required PUSHes and POPs *inside* the procedure, so you don't have to write those instructions every time you call it. Hence, for the preceding example, the four PUSHes should be the first four instructions in the CLOBBER procedure and the four POPs should be the last four instructions in CLOBBER. This lets you simply

CALL CLOBBER each time you need it, without worrying about which registers are destroyed and which are preserved.

3.5 Arithmetic Instructions

The 8086 can perform arithmetic operations on signed or unsigned binary numbers and unsigned decimal numbers (either packed or unpacked). As Table 3–4 shows, there are instructions for the four standard arithmetic functions—addition, subtraction, multiplication, and division—and two additional instructions that "sign-extend" operands, letting you operate on mixed-size data. Before discussing the instructions themselves, we should look at the formats of the various data types.

Arithmetic Data Formats

Binary Numbers

Binary numbers may be 8 or 16 bits long, and may be either unsigned or signed. In an *unsigned* number, all 8 or 16 bits represent data. Therefore, unsigned numbers can range from 0 to 255 (8 bits) or 65,535 (16 bits). In a *signed* number, the high-order bit—Bit 7 or Bit 15—tells you the sign of the number; all other bits hold data. Therefore, signed numbers can range from 127 to −128 (8 bits) or from 32,767 to −32,768 (16 bits).

Decimal Numbers

Decimal numbers are stored as unsigned byte-size values in either "packed" or "unpacked" form. In a packed decimal number, each byte holds two *binary-coded decimal (BCD)* digits, with the most-significant digit in the upper 4 bits and the least-significant digit in the lower 4 bits. Therefore, a packed decimal byte can hold values from 00 to 99.

In an unpacked decimal number, each byte holds just one BCD digit, in the lower 4 bits. Therefore, an unpacked decimal byte can hold values only from 0 to 9. The upper 4 bits must be zero for multiplication and division, but may be any value for addition or subtraction.

How does the 8086 know *which* kind of data you are operating on? For instance, if you add 2 bytes, how does it know whether they are signed binary numbers, unsigned binary numbers, packed decimal numbers, or unpacked decimal numbers? The 8086 doesn't know what kind of data you're using, nor does it care. It treats *all* operands as binary numbers.

This approach is fine if your operands are indeed binary, but if they

Table 3–4. Arithmetic instructions.

Mnemonic		Assembler Format	OF	DF	IF	TF	SF	ZF	AF	PF	CF
									Flags		
ADDITION											
ADD	ADD	destination,source	*	—	—	—	*	*	*	*	*
ADC	ADC	destination,source	*	—	—	—	*	*	*	*	*
AAA	AAA		?	—	—	—	?	?	*	?	*
DAA	DAA		?	—	—	—	*	*	*	*	*
INC	INC	destination	*	—	—	—	*	*	*	*	—
SUBTRACTION											
SUB	SUB	destination,source	*	—	—	—	*	*	*	*	*
SBB	SBB	destination,source	*	—	—	—	*	*	*	*	*
AAS	AAS		?	—	—	—	?	?	*	?	*
DAS	DAS		?	—	—	—	*	*	*	*	*
DEC	DEC	destination	*	—	—	—	*	*	*	*	—
NEG	NEG	destination	*	—	—	—	*	*	*	*	*
CMP	CMP	destination,source	*	—	—	—	*	*	*	*	*
MULTIPLICATION											
MUL	MUL	source	*	—	—	—	?	?	?	?	*
IMUL	IMUL	source	*	—	—	—	?	?	?	?	*
AAM	AAM		?	—	—	—	*	*	?	*	?
DIVISION											
DIV	DIV	source	?	—	—	—	?	?	?	?	?
IDIV	IDIV	source	?	—	—	—	?	?	?	?	?
AAD	AAD		?	—	—	—	*	*	?	*	?
SIGN-EXTENSION											
CBW	CBW		—	—	—	—	—	—	—	—	—
CWD	CWD		—	—	—	—	—	—	—	—	—

Note: * means changed, — means unchanged, and ? means undefined.

happen to be decimal, the results will obviously be incorrect. To compensate, the 8086 has a group of "adjust" instructions that make decimal operations give the proper result. We will discuss these instructions at the appropriate places in this section.

How Numbers Are Stored in Memory

The 8086 stores 16-bit numbers in the opposite order you might expect: with the least-significant byte at the lower address. For example, in storing 1234H at a location called NUM, it puts 34H at NUM and 12H at the next byte, NUM + 1. Keep this convoluted storage scheme in mind when you display (or "dump") the contents of memory. Just remember "low data, low address; high data, high address."

Addition Instructions

Add (ADD) and Add with Carry (ADC)

The ADD and ADC instructions can add either 8- or 16-bit operands. ADD adds a source operand to a destination operand and puts the result in the destination. Symbolically, this can be represented as

```
destination = destination + source
```

ADC does the same thing as ADD, except it includes the Carry Flag (CF) in the addition, like this:

```
destination = destination + source + Carry
```

You may not be familiar with the concept of *carry* as applied to computers, but you have certainly encountered it before in adding decimal numbers with pencil and paper. For instance, this decimal addition produces two carries:

```
  98
  13
+ 79
 190
```

Adding the "ones" column produces an excess of 2, which is carried into the "tens" position. Then adding *that* column, along with the carry, generates another carry (1) which goes into the "hundreds" column. A carry is produced whenever a column cannot hold the sum of all the numbers in it.

Similarly, in a binary addition, the computer generates a carry whenever the destination operand cannot hold a sum. For instance, we know that an 8-bit register can hold unsigned values only between 0 and 255 (decimal). If we perform a binary addition of 250 and 10, we get

```
  1111 1010    (Binary representation of 250)
 +0000 1010    (Binary representation of 10)
1 0000 0100    (Answer = 260 decimal)
```

The sum is correct, but it takes nine bit positions to represent it! If we are using 8-bit registers, the lower 8 bits are returned in the destination register, and the ninth bit is returned in the *Carry Flag (CF)*.

Now you see why the 8086 has two separate add instructions. One instruction, ADD, can add single-byte or single-word numbers and the low-order terms of multi-precision numbers. The other, ADC, is used to add the higher-order terms of two multi-precision numbers.

For example, the instruction

```
ADD AX,CX
```

adds the 16-bit contents of AX and CX, and returns the result in AX. If your operands are longer than 16 bits, you can use this kind of sequence:

```
ADD  AX,CX     ;Add low-order 16 bits,
ADC  BX,DX     ; then high-order 16 bits
```

which adds the 32-bit number in CX and DX to the 32-bit number in AX and BX. Here, the ADC instruction includes any carry out of (CX)+(AX) into (BX)+(DX).

You may also add a memory operand to a general register (or vice versa), or add an immediate value to a register or to memory. The following forms are legal:

```
ADD  AX,MEM_WORD   ;Add a memory operand to a
ADD  MEM_WORD,AX   ; register or vice versa
ADD  AL,10         ;Add a constant to a register
ADD  MEM_BYTE,0FH  ; or to a memory location
```

Most combinations are legal, but you may not add memory to memory, nor may you use an immediate value as a destination.

ADD and ADC can affect six flags:

- The Carry Flag (CF) is 1 if the result cannot be contained in the destination operand; otherwise, CF is 0.
- The Parity Flag (PF) is 1 if the result has an even number of 1 bits; otherwise, PF is 0.
- The Auxiliary Carry Flag (AF) is 1 if the result of a decimal addition needs to be adjusted; otherwise, AF is 0.
- The Zero Flag (ZF) is 1 if the result is zero; otherwise, ZF is 0.
- The Sign Flag (SF) is 1 if the high-order bit of the result is a 1; otherwise, SF is 0.
- The Overflow Flag (OF) is 1 if adding two like-signed numbers (both positive or both negative) gives a result that exceeds the twos-complement range of the destination, which changes the sign; otherwise, OF is 0.

The statuses of SF and OF are pertinent only when you add signed numbers. The status of AF is pertinent only when you add decimal numbers.

The 8086 has instructions that test flags and base an execution decision on the outcome. For instance, a negative result may cause one set of instructions to execute and a non-negative result may cause an alternate set of instructions to execute. We discuss these "decision-making" instructions later in the chapter.

ASCII and Decimal Adjust for Addition (AAA and DAA)

As we mentioned previously, the 8086 performs all additions as if the operands are binary. What happens if your operands are binary-coded decimal (BCD) numbers? Let's find out by looking at an example. If you add the packed BCD numbers 26 and 55, the 8086 performs this binary addition:

```
  0010 0110  (= BCD 26)
 +0101 0101  (= BCD 55)
  0111 1011  (= ??)
```

Instead of the correct answer—BCD 81—the result has a high digit of 7 and a low digit of hexadecimal B. Does this mean you can't add decimal numbers with the 8088? No, it means that you must *adjust* the result, to put it into BCD form.

The instructions ASCII Adjust for Addition (AAA) and Decimal Adjust for Addition (DAA) adjust the result of a decimal addition. Neither instruction takes an operand, but both assume that the result to be adjusted is in the AL register.

The AAA instruction converts the contents of AL to an *unpacked* decimal digit. Briefly, AAA examines the low 4 bits of AL. If these bits hold a valid BCD digit (a value between 0 and 9), AAA clears the high 4 bits of AL and the flags AF and CF. If, however, the low 4 bits of AL hold a value greater than 9, or if AF is set to 1, AAA adjusts the result as follows:

1. Add 6 to the AL register.
2. Add 1 to the AH register.
3. Set AF and CF to 1.
4. Clear the high 4 bits of AL.

In Step 1, AAA adds 6 to AL because adding 6 to any hexadecimal digit between A and F produces a value between 0 and 5 (valid BCD digits) in the low 4 bits of the result.

You use AAA instruction in this kind of sequence:

```
ADD AL,BL  ;Add unpacked BCD numbers in AL and BL
AAA        ; and make the result an unpacked
           ; number
```

The result in AL is always a valid BCD digit, but now you know that if CF is 1, AH has been incremented to reflect a too-large result.

AAA updates CF and AF and leaves PF, ZF, SF, and OF undefined. AF and CF tell you whether the result is greater than 9. If CF is 1, you need an additional byte to hold the excess digit.

The DAA instruction converts the value in AL to two *packed* decimal digits. DAA operates similar to AAA, but DAA must consider two separate digits. Here is what DAA does:

1. If the low 4 bits of AL hold a value greater than 9, or if *AF* is 1, DAA adds 6 to AL and sets AF to 1.

2. If the high 4 bits of AL hold a value greater than 9, or if *CF* is 1, DAA adds 60H to AL and sets CF to 1.

The DAA instruction is used in this kind of sequence:

```
ADD AL,BL   ;Add packed BCD numbers in AL and
            ; BL
DAA         ; and make the result a packed
            ; number
```

Again, the result in AL is always valid, but if CF is 1, you need an additional byte to hold an excess BCD digit.

DAA updates CF, PF, AF, ZF, and SF and leaves OF undefined. Only CF is pertinent, however, because it tells you whether the result exceeds the packed BCD limit, 99. Assume that the five other statuses are destroyed.

Increment Destination by One (INC)

The INC instruction adds 1 to a register or memory operand but, unlike ADD, does not affect the Carry Flag (CF). INC is often used in repetitive loop operations, to update a counter. It can also be applied to an index register or pointer when you are accessing consecutive locations in memory. You cannot increment a segment register, however.

Some examples of INC are:

```
INC   CX               ;Increment a word register
INC   AL               ; or a byte register
INC   MEM_BYTE         ;Increment a byte in memory
INC   MEM_WORD[BX]     ; or a word in memory
```

Interestingly, the 8086 takes longer to increment an 8-bit register than it does a 16-bit register (see INC entry in Appendix C)! This happens because the Intel designers assumed that programmers would use word-size counters more than byte-size counters, so they provided a special, one-byte version of INC for 16-bit registers.

Subtraction Instructions

How the 8086 Subtracts

Like every other general-purpose microprocessor, the 8086 has no internal unit that subtracts. Does that mean you can skip this section? No! Although the 8086 has no subtraction unit, it *does* have an internal *addition* unit—an adder—and can subtract numbers by adding them.

Strange as this seems, the concept is quite "elementary," as Mr. Holmes says.

To see how you can subtract by adding, consider how you subtract 7 from 10. In elementary school you learned to write this as

```
10 - 7
```

Later (in Algebra 101, perhaps), you learned that another way to write this operation is

```
10 + (-7)
```

The first form—the straight subtraction—could be performed by a processor that has a subtraction unit. Since the 8086 has no such unit, it performs the subtraction in two steps. First, it negates, or *complements*, the subtrahend (the second number). This done, it adds the minuend and complemented subtrahend to produce the result. Because the 8086 works with base 2 (binary) numbers, the complement is a *twos*-complement.

To obtain the twos-complement of a binary number, you take the positive form of the number and reverse the sense of each bit (change each 1 to 0 and each 0 to 1), then add 1 to the result.

Applying this to our "10 − 7" example, the 8-bit binary representations of 10 and 7 are 00001010B and 00000111B, respectively. Take the twos-complement of 7 as follows:

```
  1111 1000 (Reverse all bits)
+          1 (Add 1)
  1111 1001 (twos-complement of 7 or -7)
```

Now, the subtraction operation becomes

```
  0000 1010 (= 10)
+1111 1001 (= -7)
  0000 0011 (Answer = 3)
```

Eureka! We got the right answer!

Since the 8086 does the twos-complementing automatically, there aren't many occasions when you will want to do it yourself. Later in this section, however, we will study an instruction called NEG that performs a twos-complement, in case you ever need it.

Subtract (SUB) and Subtract with Borrow (SBB)

SUB and SBB are similar to their addition counterparts (ADD and ADC), but with subtraction, the Carry Flag (CF) acts as a *borrow* indicator. SUB subtracts a source operand from a destination operand and returns the result in the destination. That is,

```
destination = destination - source
```

SBB does the same thing, except it also subtracts out the Carry Flag (CF), like this:

```
destination = destination - source - Carry
```

As with addition, the subtraction instructions perform two separate functions. One instruction, SUB, subtracts single-byte or single-word numbers, or subtracts the low-order terms of multiprecision numbers. The other, SBB, subtracts the higher-order terms of two multiprecision numbers.

For example, the instruction

```
SUB AX,CX
```

subtracts the contents of CX from the contents of AX, and returns the result in AX.

If your operands are longer than 16 bits, you can use this kind of sequence:

```
SUB AX,CX ;Subtract low-order 16 bits
SBB BX,DX ; then high-order 16 bits
```

This sequence subtracts the 32-bit number in CX and DX from the 32-bit number in AX and BX. The SBB instruction includes any borrow out of the first subtraction when it subtracts DX from BX.

You may also subtract a memory operand from a register (or vice versa), or subtract an immediate value from a register or a memory location. The following forms are legal:

```
SUB   AX,MEM_WORD       ;Subtract memory from a
SUB   MEM_WORD[BX],AX   ; register or vica versa
SUB   AL,10             ;Subtract constant from a
SUB   MEM_BYTE,0FH      ; register or from a
                       ; memory location
```

You may not subtract one memory value from another directly, nor may you use an immediate value as a destination.

SUB and SBB can affect six flags:

- The Carry Flag (CF) is 1 if a borrow was needed; otherwise, CF is 0.
- The Parity Flag (PF) is 1 if the result has an even number of 1 bits; otherwise, PF is 0.
- The Auxiliary Carry Flag (AF) is 1 if the result of a decimal subtraction needs to be adjusted; otherwise, AF is 0.

- The Zero Flag (ZF) is 1 if the result is zero; otherwise, ZF is 0.
- The Sign Flag (SF) is 1 if the high-order bit of the result is 1; otherwise, SF is 0.
- The Overflow Flag (OF) is 1 if you subtract a positive number from a negative number (or vice versa) and the result exceeds the twos-complement range of the destination, which changes the sign; otherwise, OF is 0.

The statuses of SF or OF are pertinent only when you subtract signed numbers. The status of AF is pertinent only when you subtract decimal numbers.

ASCII and Decimal Adjust for Subtraction (AAS and DAS)

As with addition, the 8086 subtracts as if the operands are binary numbers. This means that your answers may be incorrect if you are subtracting binary-coded decimal (BCD) numbers. For example, suppose you want to subtract BCD 26 from BCD 55. The 8086 would perform a binary subtraction by taking the twos-complement of 26, then perform this addition:

```
   0101  0101  (= BCD 55)
  +1101  1010  (= twos-complement of BCD 26)
 1 0010  1111  (= ??)
```

Instead of the correct answer—BCD 29—the result has a high digit of 2, a low digit of hexadecimal F, and a carry. Clearly, this result sorely needs adjusting.

The instructions ASCII Adjust for Subtraction (AAS) and Decimal Adjust for Subtraction (DAS) adjust the result after you subtract two decimal numbers. Neither instruction takes an operand, but both assume that the number to adjust is in the AL register.

The AAS instruction converts the contents of AL to a valid *unpacked* decimal digit. Briefly, AAS examines the low 4 bits of AL. If these bits hold a valid BCD digit (a value between 0 and 9), AAS clears the high 4 bits of AL and the AF and CF flags. If, however, the low 4 bits of AL hold a value greater than 9, or if AF is set to 1, AAS performs the following adjustment procedure:

1. Subtract 6 from the AL register.
2. Subtract 1 from the AH register.
3. Set AF and CF to 1.
4. Clear the high 4 bits of AL.

In Step 1, AAS subtracts 6 from AL because subtracting 6 from any hexadecimal digit between A and F produces a value between 4 and 9 (valid BCD digits) in the low 4 bits of the result.

You use AAS in this kind of sequence:

```
SUB AL,BL  ;Subtract BCD number in BL from AL
AAS        ;and make the result an unpacked
           ; number
```

The result in AL is always a valid BCD digit, but if CF is 1, you know AH has been decremented to reflect a too-small result.

AAS updates CF and AF and leaves PF, ZF, SF, and OF undefined. AF and CF tell you whether the result is larger than 9. If CF is 1, you need an additional byte to hold the entire result.

The DAS instruction converts the contents of AL to two *packed* decimal digits. The operation of DAS is similar to that of AAS, but two separate digits must be considered. Here is what DAS does:

1. If the low 4 bits of AL hold a value greater than 9, or if *AF* is 1, DAS subtracts 6 from the AL register and sets AF to 1.
2. If the high 4 bits of AL hold a value greater than 9, or if *CF* is 1, DAS subtracts 60H from the AL register and sets CF to 1.

You use DAS in this kind of sequence:

```
SUB AL,BL  ;Subtract packed BCD number in BL from
DAS        ; AL and make the result a packed
           ;  number
```

Again, the result in AL is always valid, but if CF is 1, you need an additional byte to hold the complete result.

DAS updates CF, PF, AF, ZF, and SF and leaves OF underfined. Only CF is pertinent, however, because it tells you whether the result is larger than the packed BCD limit, 99. Assume that the five other statuses are destroyed.

Decrement Destination by One (DEC)

The DEC instruction subtracts 1 from a register or memory operand, but unlike SUB, does not affect the Carry Flag (CF). DEC is often used in loops to decrement a counter until the count becomes zero or negative. It can also be applied to an index register or pointer when you access consecutive locations in memory. You cannot decrement a segment register, however.

Some examples of DEC are:

```
DEC CX           ;Decrement a word register
DEC AL           ; or a byte register
DEC MEM_BYTE     ;Decrement a byte in memory
DEC MEM_WORD[BX] ; or a word in memory
```

Negate (NEG)

The NEG instruction subtracts the destination operand from zero, thereby forming the operand's twos-complement.

NEG affects the flags in the same way as SUB. Since one operand is zero, however, we can be more explicit about the conditions that set individual flags. Therefore, for NEG:

- The Carry Flag (CF) and the Sign Flag (SF) are 1 if the operand is a nonzero positive number; otherwise, CF and SF are 0.
- The Parity Flag (PF) is 1 if the result has an even number of 1 bits; otherwise, PF is 0.
- The Zero Flag (ZF) is 1 if the operand is zero; otherwise, ZF is 0.
- The Oveflow Flag (OF) is 1 if the operand has the value 80H (byte) or 8000H (word); otherwise, OF is 0.

NEG is useful for subtracting a register or memory operand from an immediate value. For instance, you may want to subtract the contents of AL from 100. Since an immediate value can't serve as a destination, the form SUB 100,AL is illegal. As an alternative, you can negate AL and *add* 100 to the result, like this:

```
NEG AL
ADD AL,100
```

Compare Destination to Source (CMP)

Most programs don't execute all instructions in the order they are stored in memory. Instead, they usually include jumps, loops, procedure calls, and other factors that make the 8086 transfer from one place to another in memory. We will discuss the instructions that actually produce these transfers later in this chapter, when we discuss the 8086's control transfer instructions. At this point we will discuss the CMP instruction, which is commonly used to configure the flags on which the control transfer instructions base their transfer/no-transfer "decisions."

CMP acts very much like the SUB instruction. That is, CMP subtracts a source operand from a destination operand, and sets or clears certain flags based on the result (see Table 3–5). But unlike SUB, *CMP does not save the result of the subtraction.*

That is, CMP doesn't alter the operands. CMP's sole purpose is to set up the flags for decision making by conditional jump instructions.

Multiplication Instructions

Multiply, Unsigned (MUL) and Integer Multiply, Signed (IMUL)

If you have ever endured the agony of writing a multiplication program for the 8080, 6502, or any other conventional 8-bit microprocessor,

Table 3–5. CMP instruction results.

Condition	OF	SF	ZF	CF
Unsigned Operands				
Source < Destination	D	D	0	0
Source = Destination	D	D	1	0
Source > Destination	D	D	0	1
Signed Operands				
Source < Destination	0/1	0	0	D
Source = Destination	0	0	1	D
Source > Destination	0/1	1	0	D

Note: "D" means Don't Care; "0/1" means the flag may be either 0 or 1, depending on the values of the operands.

you will be glad to hear that the 8086 has built-in multiplication instructions.

Multiply (MUL) multiplies unsigned numbers and Integer Multiply (IMUL) multiplies signed numbers. Both can multiply bytes or words.

These instructions have the general forms

```
MUL    source
IMUL   source
```

where *source* is a byte- or word-length general register or memory location. For the second operand, MUL and IMUL use the contents of the accumulator: AL for byte operations and AX for word operations. The double-length products are returned as follows:

- A *byte* multiplication returns the 16-bit product in AH (high byte) and AL (low byte).
- A *word* multiplication returns the 32-bit product in DX (high word) and AX (low word).

Upon completion, the Carry Flag (CF) and the Overflow Flag (OF) tell you how much of the product is relevant. For MUL, if the high-order half of the product is zero, CF and OF are 0; otherwise, they are 1. For IMUL, if the high-order half of the product is just a sign-extension of the low-order half, CF and OF are 0; otherwise, they are 1.

Here are some multiplication examples:

```
MUL    BX          ;Unsigned multiply of BX times AX
MUL    MEM_BYTE    ;Unsigned multiply of memory
                   ; times AL
IMUL DL            ;Signed multiply of DL times AL
IMUL MEM_WORD      ;Signed multiply of memory times
                   ; AX
```

Note that neither MUL nor IMUL lets you multiply by an immediate value directly. To do this, you must put the immediate value into a register or a memory location. For example,

```
MOV DX,10
MUL DX
```

multiplies AX by 10.

ASCII Adjust for Multiplication (AAM)

The AAM instruction converts the product of a preceding byte multiplication into two valid unpacked decimal operands. It assumes that the double-length product is in AH and AL, and returns the unpacked operands in AH and AL. For AAM to work correctly, the original multiplier and multiplicand must have been valid unpacked operands.

To make the conversion, AAM divides the AL register by 10 and stores the resulting quotient and remainder in AH and AL, respectively. It also updates the Parity Flag (PF), the Zero Flag (ZF), and the Sign Flag (SF) to reflect the contents of AL. The statuses of the Carry Flag (CF), Auxiliary Carry Flag (AF), and Overflow Flag (OF) are undefined.

To see how AAM works, assume AL contains 9 (00001001B) and BL contains 7 (00000111B). The instruction

```
MUL BL
```

multiplies AL by BL and returns a 16-bit result in AH and AL. In this case, it returns 0 in AH and 00111111B (decimal 63) in AL.

The subsequent instruction

```
AAM
```

divides AL by 10 and returns a quotient of 00000110B in AH and a remainder of 00000011B in AL. This double-length result is indeed correct—BCD 63, in unpacked form.

The 8086 has no instruction that multiplies *packed* decimal numbers. If you want to multiply such numbers, you must unpack them (with AAM), multiply, then pack the result.

Division Instructions

Divide, Unsigned (DIV) and Integer Divide, Signed (IDIV)

Just as the 8086 has two separate multiplication instructions, it also

has two separate division instructions. Divide (DIV) performs an unsigned division and Integer Divide (IDIV) performs a signed division.

These instructions have the general forms

```
DIV   source
IDIV  source
```

where *source* is a byte- or word-length divisor in a general register or a
memory location. The dividend is a double-length operand in either AH
and AL (8-bit operation) or DX and AX (16-bit operation). The results
are as follows:

- If the source operand is a *byte*, the quotient is returned in AL and the
  remainder in AH.
- If the source operand is a *word*, the quotient is returned in AX and the
  remainder in DX.

Both instructions leave the flags undefined, but if the quotient cannot
fit in the destination register (AL or AX), the 8086 has a dramatic way
of telling you the result is invalid: it generates a *type 0 (divide by 0)
interrupt*.

The following conditions cause a divide overflow:

1. The divisor is zero.
2. For an unsigned byte divide, the dividend is at least 256 times larger than
   the divisor.
3. For an unsigned word divide, the dividend is at least 65,536 times larger
   than the divisor.
4. For a signed byte divide, the quotient exceeds +127 or −128.
5. For a signed word divide, the quotient exceeds +32,767 or −32,768.

Here are some typical division operations:

```
DIV    BX          ;Divide DX:AX by BX, unsigned
DIV    MEM_BYTE     ;Divide AH:AL by memory,
                    ; unsigned
IDIV   DL           ;Divide AH:AL by DL, signed
IDIV   MEM_WORD     ;Divide BX:AX by memory, signed
```

Note that neither DIV nor IDIV lets you divide by an immediate value
directly. To do this, you must put the immediate value into a register
or memory location. For instance,

```
MOV BX,20
DIV BX
```

divides DX:AX by 20.

ASCII Adjust for Division (AAD)

The decimal adjust instructions we previously described—AAA, DAA, AAS, DAS, and AAM—all operate on the *result* of an operation. By contrast, you apply the AAD instruction *before* you execute a division operation.

AAD converts an unpacked dividend to a binary value in AL. To do this, it multiplies the high-order digit of the dividend (the contents of AH) by 10 and adds the result to the low-order digit in AL. Then it zeroes the contents of AH.

This sequence shows a typical use of AAD:

```
AAD          ;Adjust the unpacked dividend in AH:AL
DIV  BL      ; then perform the division
```

Sign-Extension Instructions

Two instructions let you operate on mixed-size data, by doubling the length of a signed operand. Convert Byte to Word (CBW) reproduces Bit 7 of AL throughout AH. Convert Word to Doubleword (CWD) reproduces Bit 15 of AX throughout DX. Figure 3–7 illustrates these operations.

Thus, CBW lets you add a byte to a word, subtract a word from a byte, and so forth. Similarly, CWD lets you divide a word by a word. Here are some examples:

```
CBW          ;Add a byte in AL to a word in BX
ADD    AX,BX
CBW          ;Multiply a byte in AL by a word in
             ; BX
IMUL  BX
CWD          ;Divide a word in AX by a word in BX
IDIV  BX
```

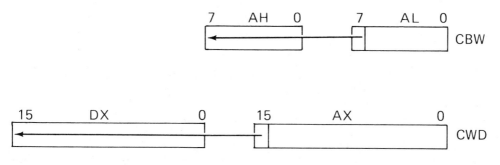

Figure 3–7. How CBW and CWD sign-extend data.

3.6 Bit Manipulation Instructions

These instructions manipulate bit patterns within registers and memory locations. Table 3–6 divides them into three groups: logical, shift, and rotate.

Logical Instructions

Logical instructions are so named because they operate according to the rules of formal logic, rather than the rules of mathematics. For example, the rule of logic stated

```
If A is true and B is true, then C is true
```

has an 8086 counterpart in the AND instruction, which applies this rule to corresponding bits in two operands.

Specifically, for each bit position where both operands have a 1 (true) state, AND sets the corresponding bit in the destination operand to 1. Conversely, for any bit position where the two operands have any other

Table 3–6. Bit manipulation instructions.

Mnemonic	Assembler Format		OF	DF	IF	TF	SF	ZF	AF	PF	CF
						Flags					
		LOGICAL									
AND	AND	destination,source	0	—	—	—	*	*	?	*	0
OR	OR	destination,source	0	—	—	—	*	*	?	*	0
XOR	XOR	destination,source	0	—	—	—	*	*	?	*	0
NOT	NOT	destination	—	—	—	—	—	—	—	—	—
TEST	TEST	destination,source	0	—	—	—	*	*	?	*	0
		SHIFT									
SAL/SHL	SAL	destination,count	*	—	—	—	*	*	?	*	*
SAR	SAR	destination,count	*	—	—	—	*	*	?	*	*
SHR	SHR	destination,count	*	—	—	—	0	*	?	*	*
		ROTATE									
ROL	ROL	destination,count	*	—	—	—	—	—	—	—	*
ROR	ROR	destination,count	*	—	—	—	—	—	—	—	*
RCL	RCL	destination,count	*	—	—	—	—	—	—	—	*
RCR	RCR	destination,count	*	—	—	—	—	—	—	—	*

Note: * mean changed, — means unchanged, and ? means undefined.

Table 3–7. Hexadecimal values for bit positions.

Bit Number	Hexadecimal Value	Bit Number	Hexadecimal Value
0	0001	8	0100
1	0002	9	0200
2	0004	10	0400
3	0008	11	0800
4	0010	12	1000
5	0020	13	2000
6	0040	14	4000
7	0080	15	8000

combination—both are 0 or one is 0 and the other is 1—AND sets the bit in the destination to 0.

Since logical operations reference bits within an operand, you usually use hexadecimal numbering for the operands. The 8086's logical instructions can operate on either bytes or words, so you normally deal with either two or four hexadecimal digits.

To help you construct the correct "mask" value for a logical operation, Table 3–7 shows the hexadecimal representation of a 1 in 16 different bit positions. For example, to operate on Bit 2, the correct mask value is 4H; to operate on Bits 2 and 3, the mask is 0CH (hex 4 + hex 8); and so on.

Logical AND (AND), Inclusive-OR (OR), and Exclusive-OR (XOR)

You already encountered AND, OR, and XOR in Section 2.7, when we discussed logical operators of the same names. Operators do their work when the program is *assembled,* however, while instructions do theirs when the program is *executed.* Still, these operators and instructions have the same names because they function in the same way. Although we describe the AND, OR, and XOR instructions here for the sake of completeness, you might want to refer to Section 2.7 for explanations of how they operate.

The AND, OR, and XOR instructions can be applied to byte or word operands, and let you combine two registers, a register with a memory location, or an immediate value with a register or a memory location. Table 3–8 shows what effect these instructions have.

The *AND* instruction masks out (zeroes) certain bits in a number so that we can do some kind of processing on the remaining bits. As just mentioned, for each bit position in which both operands contain 1, the

Table 3–8. The AND, OR, and XOR bit combinations.

Source	Destination	Result AND	OR	XOR
0	0	0	0	0
0	1	0	1	1
1	0	0	1	1
1	1	1	1	0

corresponding bit position in the destination is also 1. All other operand bit combinations put a 0 in the destination bit. Note that *any bit ANDed with 0 becomes 0, and any bit ANDed with 1 retains its original value.*
Some examples of AND are:

```
AND  AX,BX          ;AND two registers
AND  AL,MEM_BYTE    ;AND register with memory
AND  MEM_BYTE,AL    ; or vice versa
AND  BL,1101B       ;AND a constant with a
AND  TABLE[BX],MASK3 ; register or with memory
```

To see how AND works, suppose Port 200 is connected to the 16-bit status register of an external device in the system, and Bit 6 indicates whether that device's power is on (1) or off (0). If your program requires device power to be on before continuing, it might include the following loop:

```
CHK_PWR:  IN   AX,200         ;Read device status
          AND  AX,1000000B    ;Isolate the power
                              ; indicator
          JZ   CHK_PWR        ;Wait until power is
          ..                  ; on, then continue
          ..
```

The JZ (Jump if Zero) instruction, which we have not yet discussed, makes the 8086 jump back to the IN instruction at CHK_PWR if the Zero Flag (ZF) is 1, and continue to the next instruction otherwise. Here, ZF is 1 only when the power indicator—Bit 6— is 1, because the AND instruction already zeroed the other bits in AX.
The *OR* instruction produces a 1 result in the destination for each bit position in which either or both operands contain 1. OR is usually used to force specific bits to 1. For example,

```
OR BX,0C000H
```

sets the two most-significant bits (14 and 15) of BX to 1 and leaves all other bits unchanged.
The *XOR* instruction is used primarily to determine which bits differ

between two operands, but it can also be used to reverse the state of selected bits. XOR produces a 1 in the destination for every bit position in which the operands differ, that is, for every bit position in which one operand has 0 and the other has 1. If both operands contain either 0 or 1, XOR clears the destination bit to 0.

For example,

```
XOR BX,0C000H
```

reverses the state of the two most-significant bits of BX (14 and 15) and leaves all other bits unchanged.

Logical NOT (NOT)

The NOT instruction reverses the state of each bit in its register or memory operand, without affecting any flags. That is, NOT changes each 1 to 0 and each 0 to 1. Thus, we say that NOT takes the *ones-complement* of an operand.

Test (TEST)

The TEST instruction logically ANDs the source and destination operands, but affects only the flags; it doesn't alter either operand. TEST affects the flags the same as AND: it clears CF and OF to 0, updates PF, ZF, and SF, and leaves AF undefined.

If you follow TEST with a JNZ (Jump if Not Zero) instruction, the jump will be taken if there are any corresponding 1 bits in both operands.

Shift and Rotate Instructions

The 8086 has seven instructions that displace the 8- or 16-bit contents of a general register or memory location one or more positions to the left or right. Three of these instructions "shift" the operand, the other four "rotate" it.

For all seven instructions, the Carry Flag (CF) acts as a "9th bit" or "17th bit" extension of the operand, in that CF receives the value of the bit that has been displaced out of one end of the operand. A right shift or rotate puts the value of Bit 0 into CF. A left shift or rotate puts the value of Bit 7 (byte) or Bit 15 (word) into CF.

Shift and rotate instructions fall into two groups. *Logical* instructions displace an operand without regard to its sign. You use them to operate on unsigned numbers and non-numbers such as masks. *Arithmetic* instructions preserve the most-significant bit of the operand, the sign bit. You use them to operate on signed numbers. Figure 3–8 shows how the various shift and rotate instructions operate.

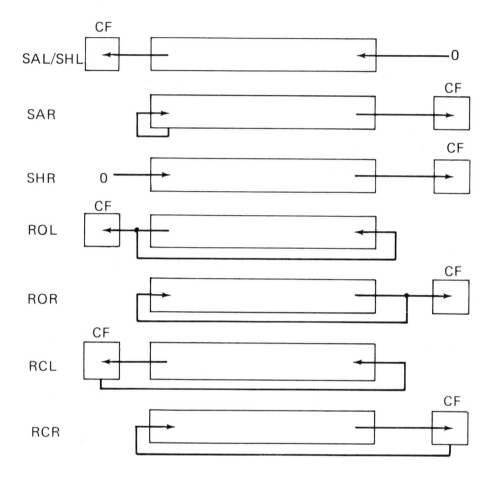

Figure 3–8. Shift and rotate operations.

The shift and rotate instructions take two operands: a *destination* and a *count*. The destination may be a general register or a memory location of either byte or word length. The count may be "1" or an unsigned value in the CL register.

Shift Instructions

Shift Arithmetic Left (SAL) and *Shift Arithmetic Right (SAR)* shift signed numbers. SAR preserves the sign of the operand by replicating the sign bit throughout the shift operation. SAL does not preserve the sign bit, but it does put 1 in the Overflow Flag (OF) if the sign ever changes. Each time SAL shifts an operand, the vacated Bit 0 position receives 0.

Shift Logical Left (SHL) and *Shift Logical Right (SHR)* shift unsigned numbers. SHL does the same thing as SAL. SHR is similar to SHL, but it shifts operands right instead of left. Each time SHR shifts an operand, the vacated high-order bit position (Bit 7 in a byte, Bit 15 in a word) receives 0.

Besides CF and OF, the shift instructions update PF, ZF, and SF, and leave AF undefined.

To see how the shift instructions work, assume the AL register contains 0B4H and the Carry Flag is set to 1. In binary,

```
AL = 10110100   CF = 1
```

Here is how the four shift instructions affect AL and CFL

```
After SAL AL,1: AL = 01101000 CF = 1
After SAR AL,1: AL = 11011010 CF = 0
After SHL AL,1: AL = 01101000 CF = 1
After SHR AL,1: AL = 01011010 CF = 0
```

The shift instructions have a lot of miscellaneous uses. For instance, the following sequence uses SHL to convert two unpacked BCD numbers—a high digit in BL and a low digit in AL—to a packed BCD number in AL:

```
MOV    CL,4      ;Load shift count into CL
SHL    BL,CL     ;Shift high digit into high 4 bits
                 ; of BL
OR     AL,BL     ;Merge AL and BL to form packed
                 ; BCD number
```

The shift instructions also make fast-executing multiply and divide instructions, because *shifting an operand one bit position to the left doubles its value (multiplies it by two) and shifting it one bit position to the right halves its values (divides it by two).*

The following shift instructions show you how to multiply or divide the contents of AX by four. Assume CL contains 2 in all cases.

```
SHL    AX,CL     ;Multiply an unsigned number by 4
SAL    AX,CL     ;Multiply a signed number by 4
SHR    AX,CL     ;Divide an unsigned number by 4
SAR    AX,CL     ;Divide a signed number by 4
```

You save considerable time by multiplying and dividing with shift instructions rather than with the 8086's multiply and divide instructions. Each of the preceding shift instructions takes 16 clock cycles to execute. It takes four more cycles to initialize the CL register, for a total of 20 clock cycles. Compare this with the minimum execution times for MUL (118 cycles), IMUL (128 cycles), DIV (144 cycles), and IDIV (165 cycles) and you will see that the shift instructions make these calculations about *six to eight times faster* than their multiply and divide counterparts!

Of course, a single shift instruction can multiply or divide only by multiples of two, but by juggling some registers, you can multiply or divide by other factors. For example, this sequence multiplies AX by 10:

```
MOV   BX,AX     ;Save contents of AX in BX
SHL   AX,1      ;Shift AX (multiply by 2)
SHL   AX,1      ;Shift AX again (multiply by 4)
ADD   AX,BX     ;Add original AX (multiply by 5)
SHL   AX,1      ;Shift AX again (multiply by 10)
```

Even though this sequence has five instructions, it is about 11 times faster than a single MUL instruction!

Rotate Instructions

The rotate instructions are similar to the shift instructions, but rotates *preserve* displaced bits by storing them back into the operand. As with the shift instructions, bits displaced out of the operand enter the Carry Flag (CF).

For Rotate Left (ROL) and Rotate Right (ROR), the bit displaced out of one end of the operand enters the opposite end. For Rotate Left through Carry (RCL) and Rotate Right through Carry (RCR), the *previous* value of CF goes into the opposite end of the operand. The rotate instructions affect only two flags: CF and OF.

To see how the rotate instructions work, let's use the same example we used to illustrate the shift instructions:

```
AL = 10110100 CF = 1
```

Here is how the four rotate instructions would effect AL and CF:

```
After ROL AL,1: AL = 01101001 CF = 1
After ROR AL,1: AL = 01011010 CF = 0
After RCL AL,1: AL = 01101001 CF = 1
After RCR AL,1: AL = 11011010 CF = 0
```

3.7 Control Transfer Instructions

As we mentioned in our discussion of the compare instructions, program instructions are stored consecutively in memory, but programs rarely execute in that exact order. All but the simplest programs include jumps and procedure calls that alter the sequence in which the microprocessor executes the program.

The control transfer instructions can transfer program execution from one part of memory to another. As Table 3–9 shows, these instructions can be divided into three groups: unconditional transfer, conditional transfer, and iteration control. Note that the control transfer instructions do not affect the flags.

Table 3–9. Control transfer instructions.

Mnemonic	Assembler Format		OF	DF	IF	TF	SF	ZF	AF	PF	CF
			Flags								
UNCONDITIONAL TRANSFERS												
CALL	CALL	target	—	—	—	—	—	—	—	—	—
RET	RET	[pop-value]	—	—	—	—	—	—	—	—	—
JMP	JMP	target	—	—	—	—	—	—	—	—	—
CONDITIONAL TRANSFERS												
JA/JNBE	JA	short-label	—	—	—	—	—	—	—	—	—
JAE/JNB	JAE	short-label	—	—	—	—	—	—	—	—	—
JB/JNAE/JC	JB	short-label	—	—	—	—	—	—	—	—	—
JBE/JNA	JBE	short-label	—	—	—	—	—	—	—	—	—
JCXZ	JCXZ	short-label	—	—	—	—	—	—	—	—	—
JE/JZ	JE	short-label	—	—	—	—	—	—	—	—	—
JG/JNLE	JG	short-label	—	—	—	—	—	—	—	—	—
JGE/JNL	JGE	short-label	—	—	—	—	—	—	—	—	—
JL/JNGE	JL	short-label	—	—	—	—	—	—	—	—	—
JLE/JNG	JLE	short-label	—	—	—	—	—	—	—	—	—
JNC	JNC	short-label	—	—	—	—	—	—	—	—	—
JNE/JNZ	JNE	short-label	—	—	—	—	—	—	—	—	—
JNO	JNO	short-label	—	—	—	—	—	—	—	—	—
JNP/JPO	JNP	short-label	—	—	—	—	—	—	—	—	—
JNS	JNS	short-label	—	—	—	—	—	—	—	—	—
JO	JO	short-label	—	—	—	—	—	—	—	—	—
JP/JPE	JP	short-label	—	—	—	—	—	—	—	—	—
JS	JS	short-label	—	—	—	—	—	—	—	—	—
ITERATION CONTROLS												
LOOP	LOOP	short-label	—	—	—	—	—	—	—	—	—
LOOPE/LOOPZ	LOOPE	short-label	—	—	—	—	—	—	—	—	—
LOOPNE/ LOOPNZ	LOOPNE	short-label	—	—	—	—	—	—	—	—	—

Note: — means unchanged.

Unconditional Transfer Instructions

Procedures

Up to this point, the examples in this book contained instructions that perform a specific function *once*. From this you might assume that if you need to perform a specific operation at more than one place in your program, you must duplicate the entire sequence of instructions at each place you need it. Clearly, duplicating a sequence of instructions at many places in a program would be frustrating and time-consuming. It would also make programs much longer than they would be if you could avoid this duplication.

As a matter of fact, you *can* eliminate this needless duplication if you define the repeated instructions as a *procedure*. A procedure—called a subroutine in many instances—is a set of instructions that you write just once, but which you can execute as needed at any point in a program.

The process of transferring control from the main part of a program to a procedure is defined as *calling*. Thus, procedures are *called*. Once called, the 8086 executes the instructions in the procedure, then returns to the place where the call was made.

This invites two questions: "How do you call a procedure?" and "How does the 8086 return to the proper place in the program?" These questions are answered in the following discussion of two procedure-related instructions, CALL and RET.

Call a Procedure (CALL) and Return from Procedure (RET)

Instructions that execute procedures must perform three tasks:

1. They must include some provision for saving the contents of the Instruction Pointer (IP). Once the procedure has been executed, this address will be used to return the 8086 to the proper place in the program. Hence, we call it a *return address*.
2. They must cause the microprocessor to begin executing the procedure.
3. They must use the stored contents of the IP to return to the program, and continue executing at this point.

These three tasks are performed by two instructions: *Call a Procedure (CALL)* and *Return from Procedure (RET)*.

The CALL instruction performs the return address-storing and begin-executing tasks (1 and 2). The return address that CALL pushes onto the stack is 16 bits long if you defined the procedure as NEAR or 32 bits if you defined it as FAR (see Section 2.4). NEAR procedures can be called only from within the segment in which they reside; FAR procedures can be called from a different segment.

CALL has the general format

```
CALL target
```

where *target* is the name of the procedure being called. If *target* is NEAR, CALL pushes the offset address of the next instruction onto the stack. If *target* is FAR, CALL pushes the contents of the CS register, then the offset address, onto the stack.

After saving the return address on the stack, CALL loads the offset address of the target label into IP. If the procedure is FAR, CALL also loads the label's segment number into the CS register.

The RET instruction makes the 8086 leave the procedure and return to the calling program. It does this by "undoing" everything CALL did. RET must always be the last instruction in the procedure to be executed.

(This doesn't mean that RET must be the last instruction in the procedure—although it often is—but RET must be the last instruction the 8086 *executes*.)

RET pops a return address off the stack. If the called procedure is NEAR (it is in the same code segment), RET pops a 16-bit word off the stack and loads it into the Instruction Pointer (IP). If the called procedure is FAR (it is in a different code segment), RET pops *two* words off the stack: an offset address that is loaded into the IP, then a segment number that is loaded into CS.

To illustrate this, consider a NEAR procedure called MY_PROC. If your program needs to call MY_PROC at some point, it might execute the following sequence (offsets are also listed):

```
04F0              CALL MY_PROC      ;Call the procedure
04F3 NEXT         MOV  AX,BX        ;Return here after
                  ..                ; the procedure
                  ..
0500 MY_PROC PROC                   (start of procedure)
0500              MOV  CL,6         ;First instruction
                  ..                ; of procedure
                                    (additional
                  ..                instructions)
                  ..
051E             RET                ;Return to calling
                  ..                ; program
051F MY_PROC ENDP                   (end of procedure)
```

Upon executing the CALL instruction, the 8086 pushes the offset address of NEXT (04F3H) onto the stack, then loads the offset address of MY_PROC (0500H) into the Instruction Pointer (IP). Since the PROC directive has no distance operand, MY_PROC is, by default, a NEAR procedure. This means that MY_PROC is in the same code segment as the CALL instruction, so the 8086 leaves the Code Segment register (CS) as is.

Now that the IP has been changed, the 8086 begins executing at that new offset address. In our example, the first instruction happens to be

```
MOV CL,6
```

When the microprocessor finally arrives at the RET instruction, it pops the return address off the stack and puts it into IP. This makes the 8086 resume at the instruction labeled NEXT. Figure 3–9 shows the stack, the Stack Pointer (SP), and the Instruction Pointer (IP) before and after the CALL, and after RET.

Indirect Calls to Procedures

So far, we have discussed just one form of the CALL instruction, a *direct* call, in which the operand is a NEAR or FAR label in a code segment.

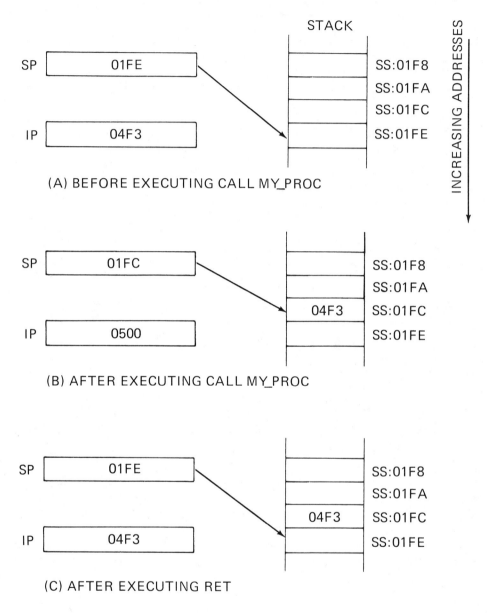

Figure 3–9. How a procedure affects the stack.

You may also make an *indirect* call to a procedure, through a register or a memory location. With indirect calls through memory, the 8086 fetches the procedure's IP value from the data segment, unless you use BP or specify an override. If you use BP to address memory, the 8086 fetches the IP value from the stack segment.

You may call a NEAR procedure through a register, like this:

```
CALL BX
```

Here, BX holds the procedure's offset address relative to CS. When the 8086 executes this instruction, it copies the contents of BX into IP, then transfers to the instruction addressed by the CS:IP combination. For example, if BX holds 1ABH, the 8086 continues executing at location 1ABH in the code segment.

You may also call a NEAR procedure through a word-size variable, as in these examples:

```
CALL WORD PTR [BX]
CALL WORD PTR [BX][SI]
CALL WORD PTR VARIABLE_NAME
CALL WORD PTR VARIABLE_NAME[BX]
CALL MEM_WORD
CALL WORD PTR ES:[BX][SI]
```

The last CALL gets its procedure address from a location in the extra segment (because of the ES override), the rest get their procedure address from a location in the data segment.

Similarly, you may call a FAR procedure indirectly through a double-word-size variable, as in these examples:

```
CALL DWORD PTR [BX]
CALL MEM_DWORD
CALL DWORD PTR SS:VARIABLE_NAME[SI]
```

Here, the first two CALLs get their procedure address from the data segment; the last gets its address from the stack segment.

How To Nest Procedures

A procedure may itself call other procedures. For instance, a subroutine that reads a keyboard character from a terminal may well decode that character and then call any of several other procedures based on the decoded result. The technique of calling a procedure from within a procedure is referred to as *nesting*. Figure 3–10 shows the CALL and RET instructions for a program in which procedure PROC_1 calls procedure PROC_1 (that is, PROC_2 is nested inside PROC_1).

Programmers usually describe nesting in terms of *levels*. An application like the one in Figure 3–10, where the nesting extends only to the CALL to PROC_2 (PROC_2 does not call another procedure), is said to have one level of nesting. There is no reason, however, why PROC_2 could not have called a third procedure (PROC_3), with PROC_3 calling PROC 4, and so on.

Considering that each CALL instruction pushes two or four address bytes onto the stack, nesting is limited only by the capacity of the stack segment. Since a stack segment can be up to 64K bytes long, your nesting capabilities are virtually unlimited.

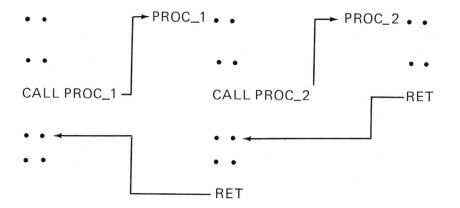

Figure 3–10. Nested procedures.

Jump Unconditionally (JMP)

Whether you know it or not, you are already familiar with the basic concepts of jump operations. Have you ever read a set of instructions for something and come across a direction like "Jump to Step 5"? Well, that's a jump operation. Similarly, when the dreaded income tax form directs you to "Go to Line 36a," that's also a jump operation.

As in these everyday situations, the JMP instruction makes the 8086 take its next instruction from some place other than the next consecutive memory location. A further similarity with everyday "jump" situations is that the JMP instruction is *unconditional*; the 8086 jumps to a new location every time it encounters a JMP.

The JMP instruction has the general form

```
JMP target
```

where *target* follows the same rules as the CALL operand. That is, *target* can be NEAR or FAR, direct or indirect. For direct jumps, the JMP instruction is 3 bytes long if the label is NEAR and 5 bytes long if it is FAR. For instance,

```
JMP THERE
```

is a 3-byte instruction if *THERE* is in the same segment or a 5-byte instruction if it is in a different segment. (For the latter case, *EXTRN THERE:FAR* must precede the segment with the JMP and *PUBLIC THERE* must precede the target segment.)

If the label lies within −128 or +127 bytes of the JMP instruction, you can force the assembler to make JMP a *2-byte* instruction by declaring the label SHORT. For example,

```
JMP SHORT NEAR_LABEL
```

is a 2-byte instruction. It executes in the same amount of time as

```
JMP NEAR_LABEL
```

but takes up one less byte in memory.

You generally use JMP to bypass a group of instructions that are executed from some other part of the program. For example, you may see JMP used like this:

```
        ..
        ..
        MOV AX,BX
        ADD DX,AX
        JMP THERE
HERE    MOV MEM_WORD,DX
        ..
        ..
THERE   MOV SAVE_DX,DX
        ..
        ..
```

Conditional Transfer Instructions

There are 17 different instructions that let the 8086 make an execution "decision" based on some prescribed condition, such as a register value being zero or CF being set to 1. If the condition is satisfied, the 8086 makes the jump; otherwise, it continues on to the next instruction in the program.

As you can see from Table 3–9 (which appeared earlier), the assembler recognizes some of these instructions by two or three different mnemonics, which are provided for your convenience. (With these alternate mnemonics, one might well claim that the 8088 has *31* conditional transfer instructions. If that's your viewpoint, you should seriously consider a career in marketing!)

For example, the assembler recognizes JA LABEL and JNBE LABEL as the same instruction. These particular instructions refer to the result of a preceding Compare (CMP) or Subtract (SUB or SBB) instruction.

The first mnemonic, JA, tells the 8086 to make the jump if the destination is "Above" (that is, greater than) the source. The second, JNBE, tells the 8086 to make the jump if the destination is "Not Below Nor Equal" to the source. JA and JNBE say exactly the same thing, but in different ways. They exist strictly for your convenience, so you can write programs that are more readily understandable.

As Table 3–9 shows, the conditional transfer instructions have the general format

```
Jx short-label
```

where x is a one- to three-letter modifier. The operand form *short-label* tells you that the target label of the jump must be no more than -128 or $+127$ bytes away from the conditional transfer instruction. (As mentioned in Chapter 2, short labels normally have a colon suffix.) Contrast this with the Jump (JMP) instruction, which can transfer anywhere in memory.

Table 3–10 summarizes the conditional transfer instructions, and shows which conditions cause a jump to occur. Here, the mnemonics are listed individually so you don't have to search through a list of alternate mnemonics.

Table 3–10. The conditional transfer instructions.

Instruction	Description	Jump If
JA	Jump If Above	CF = 0 and ZF = 0
JAE	Jump If Above or Equal	CF = 0
JB	Jump If Below	CF = 1
JBE	Jump If Below or Equal	CF = 1 or ZF = 1
JC	Jump If Carry	CF = 1
JCXZ	Jump If CX Is Zero	(CX) = 0
JE	Jump If Equal	ZF = 1
*JG	Jump If Greater	ZF = 0 and SF = OF
*JGE	Jump If Greater or Equal	SF = OF
*JL	Jump If Less	SF not = OF
*JLE	Jump If Less or Equal	ZF = 1 or SF not = OF
JNA	Jump If Not Above	CF = 1 or ZF = 1
JNAE	Jump If Not Above Nor Equal	CF = 1
JNB	Jump If Not Below	CF = 0
JNBE	Jump If Not Below Nor Equal	CF = 0 and ZF = 0
JNC	Jump If No Carry	CF = 0
JNE	Jump If Not Equal	ZF = 0
*JNG	Jump If Not Greater	ZF = 1 or SF not = OF
*JNGE	Jump If Not Greater Nor Equal	SF not = OF
*JNL	Jump If Not Less	SF = OF
*JNLE	Jump If Not Less Nor Equal	ZF = 0 and SF = OF
*JNO	Jump If No Overflow	OF = 0
JNP	Jump If No Parity (Odd)	PF = 0
*JNS	Jump If No Sign	SF = 0
JNZ	Jump If Not Zero	ZF = 0
*JO	Jump on Overflow	OF = 1
JP	Jump on Parity (Even)	PF = 1
JPE	Jump If Parity Even	PF = 1
JPO	Jump If Parity Odd	PF = 0
*JS	Jump on Sign	SF = 1
JZ	Jump If Zero	ZF = 1

*Pertinent for signed (twos-complement) arithmetic.

Conditional transfer instructions occupy 2 bytes in memory; the first byte holds the operation code and the second byte holds the relative displacement. These instructions execute in 16 clock cycles if the jump is taken, and four clock cycles if it is not taken. Because of this time differential, you should construct your programs so that, whenever possible, the expected case executes if the jump is *not taken*.

Here are a few examples of conditional transfer instructions:

1. The sequence

```
ADD AL,BL
JC  TOOBIG
```

jumps to TOOBIG if the add operation produces a carry.

2. The sequence

```
SUB AL,BL
JZ  ZERO
```

jumps to ZERO if the subtract operation produces a zero result in AL.

3. The sequence

```
CMP AL,BL
JE  ZERO
```

jumps to ZERO if AL and BL hold the same values. (The equivalent mnemonic JZ could have been used here, but JE—for "Jump if Equal"— is more explicit in this case.)

4. Some tests require you to choose between two different conditional transfer instructions, based on whether you are testing the result of a signed or unsigned operation. For example, suppose you want to jump to label BXMORE if the contents of BX are higher-valued than those of AX. The sequence

```
CMP BX,AX
JA  BXMORE
```

applies if the operands are *unsigned*, whereas

```
CMP BX,AX
JG  BXMORE
```

applies if the operands are *signed*.

Using Conditional Transfers with Compare (CMP)

Although you can precede conditional transfer instructions with any instruction that alters the flags, you normally precede them with a

Table 3–11. Using conditional transfers with Compare (CMP).

To Jump If	Follow CMP with	
	For Unsigned Numbers	For Signed Numbers
Destination is greater than Source	JA	JG
Destination is equal to Source	JE	JE
Destination is not equal to Source	JNE	JNE
Destination is less than Source	JB	JL
Destination is less than or equal to Source	JBE	JLE
Destination is greater than or equal to Source	JAE	JGE

Compare (CMP) instruction. In Table 3–5 of Section 3.5 you saw how CMP affects the flags for various source and destination relationships. Now, with the wide variety of conditional transfer instructions at your disposal, it is worthwhile to look at a more practical table—one that shows which conditional transfer to use for all possible combinations of source and destination. Table 3–11 is the one you need.

To illustrate a practical application for a conditional transfer/compare combination, Example 3–1 shows a program sequence that arranges two unsigned numbers in memory in increasing order. The data segment offsets of these numbers are assumed to be in BX and DI, respectively. Note that whenever two numbers need to be exchanged, one of them must be loaded into a register, because the 8086 has no memory-to-memory move instruction.

You can also combine a single compare instruction with two conditional transfer instructions, to test the "less than," "equal to," and

Example 3–1. Arranging Two Numbers in Increasing Order

```
; This sequence arranges two unsigned 16-bit
; numbers in memory in order of value, with the
; lower-numbered value in the lower address. The
; offset of the first number is in BX; the
; offset of the second number is in DI.
        MOV  AX,[BX]  ;Load first number into AX
        CMP  AX,[DI]  ;Compare it with second
                      ; number
        JBE  DONE     ;Is first no. below or equal
                      ; to second no.?
        XCHG AX,[DI]  ; If not, swap the two
                      ; numbers
        MOV  [BX,AX]
DONE:  ..
       ..
```

"greater than" cases separately. Example 3–2 shows a sequence that executes one of three groups of instructions, based on whether the value in AL is below, equal to, or above 10.

This sequence uses a JAE instruction to determine whether AL is above or equal to 10. If it is, the 8086 jumps to the label AE10. A JA instruction then determines whether AL is above 10. If it is, the 8086 jumps to A10. Normally, the last instruction in the first two groups would be a JMP, to skip the unused options.

Example 3–2. A Three-Way Decision Sequence

```
; This sequence causes one of three different
; groups of instructions to be executed, based
; on whether the unsigned number in AL is below,
; equal to, or above 10.
        CMP  AL,10  ;Compare AL to 10
        JAE  AE10
        ..          ;These instructions execute if
        ..          ; AL < 10
AE10: JA   A10
        ..          ;These instructions execute if
        ..          ; AL = 10
A10:  ..            ;These instructions execute if
        ..          ; AL > 10
```

Iteration Control Instructions

The iteration control instructions are conditional transfers used to set up repetitive loops. In the 8086, the Count register (CX) is designed to act as the counter for loops. Each of the iteration control instructions decrements CX by 1, then makes a jump/no-jump "decision" based on the result.

The basic instruction of this group is *Loop until Count Complete (LOOP)*. LOOP decrements CX by 1 and transfers control to a *short-label* target operand if CX is not zero. For example, to perform a certain set of operations 100 times, you might use this kind of sequence:

```
        MOV     CX,100   ;Load repetition count
                         ; into CX
START:  ..               (The instructions to be re-
                         peated to go here)

        ..
        LOOP    START    ;If CX is not zero, jump
                         ; to START
        ..               ;Otherwise, continue here
```

LOOP by itself, however, terminates the loop only if CX has been decremented to zero. Many applications involve loops that must also terminate if something takes place before CX reaches zero. The instructions that provide this alternate escape route are *Loop If Equal (LOOPE)* and *Loop If Not Equal (LOOPNE)*.

LOOPE, which has the alternate form *Loop If Zero (LOOPZ)*, decrements CX by 1, then jumps if CX is not zero and the Zero Flag (ZF) is 1. Thus, looping continues until CX is zero or ZF is 0, or both. You normally use LOOPE to find the first nonzero result in a series of operations. To illustrate, Example 3–3 shows a sequence that finds the first nonzero byte in a block of memory. The offset addresses of the first and last bytes are in BX and DI, respectively.

LOOPNE, which has the alternate form *Loop If Not Zero LOOPNZ)*, decrements CX by 1, then jumps if CX is not zero and the Zero Flag (ZF) is 0. Thus, looping continues until CX is zero or ZF is 1, or both. You normally use LOOPNE to find the first zero result in a series of operations. If you replace LOOPE with LOOPNE in Example 3–3, the sequence will find the first *zero* byte in a block of memory rather than the first nonzero byte.

Example 3–3. Find a Nonzero Location in a Memory Block

```
; This sequence finds the first nonzero byte in a
; specified block of memory. The offset of the
; starting address is in BX; the offset of the
; ending address is in DI. The offset of the
; nonzero byte is returned in BX. If no nonzero
; bytes are found, BX will hold the same value as
; DI upon return.
            SUB DI,BX              ;Byte count =
            INC DI                ; (DI) - (BX) + 1
            MOV CX,DI             ;Move byte count
                                  ; into CX

            DEC BX
NEXT:       INC BX                ;Point to next
                                  ; location

            CMP BYTE PTE [BX],0 ;and compare it to
                                  ; 0

            LOOPE NEXT            ;Go compare next
                                  ; byte

            JNZ NZ_FOUND          ;Nonzero byte
                                  ; found?
            ..                    ; No. (BX) = (DI)
NZ_FOUND:..                       ; Yes. Offset of
                                  ; the nonzero
            ..                    ; entry is in BX
```

3.8 String Instructions

The string instructions let you operate on blocks of bytes or words in memory. These blocks, or *strings*, may be up to 64K bytes long, and may consist of numeric values (either binary or BCD), alphanumeric values (such as ASCII text characters), or, for that matter, any kind of information that can be stored in memory as binary patterns.

The string instructions provide five basic operations, called *primitives*, that process strings one element (byte or word) at a time. These primitives—move, compare, scan for a value, load, and store—are summarized in Table 3–12.

As you see, each primitive has three separate instruction forms. The first form takes one or two operands (for example, MOVS takes two operands), while the other two take no operands (for example, MOVSB and MOVSW). The no-operand forms represent the instructions that the 8086 can actually execute. The assembler always converts the more general operand form to one of these two instructions when you assemble the program.

The 8086 assumes the destination string is in the extra segment and the source string is in the data segment. The processor addresses the destination string with DI and the source string with SI. For example, MOVSB copies the

Table 3–12. String instructions.

Mnemonic	Assembler Format		OF	DF	IF	TF	SF	ZF	AF	PF	CF
						Flags					
REPEAT PREFIXES											
REP	REP		—	—	—	—	—	—	—	—	—
REPE/REPZ	REPE		—	—	—	—	—	—	—	—	—
REPNE/ REPNZ	REPNE		—	—	—	—	—	—	—	—	—
MOVE											
MOVS	MOVS	dest-string, source-string	—	—	—	—	—	—	—	—	—
MOVSB	MOVSB		—	—	—	—	—	—	—	—	—
MOVSW	MOVSW		—	—	—	—	—	—	—	—	—
COMPARE											
CMPS	CMPS	dest-string, source-string	*	—	—	—	*	*	*	*	*
CMPSB	CMPSB		*	—	—	—	*	*	*	*	*
CMPSW	CMPSW		*	—	—	—	*	*	*	*	*
SCAN											
SCAS	SCAS	dest-string	*	—	—	—	*	*	*	*	*
SCASB	SCASB		*	—	—	—	*	*	*	*	*
SCASW	SCASW		*	—	—	—	*	*	*	*	*
LOAD AND STORE											
LODS	LODS	source-string	—	—	—	—	—	—	—	—	—
LODSB	LODSB		—	—	—	—	—	—	—	—	—
LODSW	LODSW		—	—	—	—	—	—	—	—	—
STOS	STOS	dest-string	—	—	—	—	—	—	—	—	—
STOSB	STOSB		—	—	—	—	—	—	—	—	—
STOSW	STOSW		—	—	—	—	—	—	—	—	—

Note: — means unchanged and * means changed.

data segment byte addressed by SI into the extra segment location addressed by DI.

Intel probably chose DI and SI here because they are easy-to-remember abbreviations for Destination Index (DI) and Source Index (SI). Clever, no?

Incidentally, although the 8086 assumes the destination string is in the extra segment and the source string is in the data segment, you *can* use other combinations. We will show you how later.

Because the string instructions are designed to operate on a *series* of elements, they automatically update the pointer(s) to address the next element in the string. For example, MOVS increments or decrements its source string pointer (SI) and destination string pointer (DI) at the end of each execution cycle.

What determines whether SI and DI increment or decrement at the end of a string instruction? It is the state of the Direction Flag (DF) bit in the 8086's Flags register. If DF is 0, SI and DI *increment* after every instruction; if DF is 1, SI and DI *decrement* after every instruction.

For example, MOVS copies an element in the source string to a location in the destination string. If DF is 0, the 8086 *increments* SI and DI after the move, thereby addressing the following element in memory. If DF is 1, the 8086 *decrements* SI and DI after the move, thereby addressing the preceding element in memory.

Two instructions let you control the state of DF: *Clear Direction Flag (CLD)* makes it 0 and *Set Direction Flags (STD)* makes it 1. We discuss CLD and STD in Section 3.10.

A single string instruction can operate on a number of consecutive elements in memory, if you precede it with a *repeat prefix* (see Table 3-12). These prefixes are not instructions, but 1-byte modifiers that cause the 8086 hardware to repeat a strong instruction. With this approach, the 8086 processes long strings much faster than it could with a software loop.

Repeat Prefixes

Repeat prefixes make the 8086 repeat a string instruction the number of times specified in the CX register. For example, the sequence

```
    MOV   CX,500
REP MOVS DEST,SOURCE
```

makes it execute the MOVS instruction 500 times (we'll discuss MOVS momentarily), and decrement the CX register after each repetition. You should interpret the REP prefix to mean "repeat while not end-of-string"; that is, repeat while CX is not 0.

The remaining repeat prefixes involve the Zero Flag (ZF) in the repeat/exit "decision," and therefore apply only to the compare string and scan string instructions, which affect ZF. Repeat while Equal (REPE), which has the alternate name Repeat while Zero (REPZ), causes the instruction to be repeated as long as ZF is 1 and CX is not zero. If you prefix a *string compare instruction (CMPS)* with REPE, the compare operation repeats until a mismatch occurs. Specifically, the sequence

```
     MOV  CX,100
 REPE CMPS DEST,SOURCE
```

compares the strings SOURCE and DEST, element by element, until 100 elements have been compared or until the 8086 finds an element in DEST that does not match the corresponding element in SOURCE.

The prefix *Repeat While Not Equal (REPNE)*, which has the alternate name Repeat While Not Zero (REPNZ), has the opposite effect of REPE. That is, REPNE causes the prefixed instruction to be repeated while ZF is 0 and CX is not zero. Therefore, the sequence

```
     MOV  CX,100
 REPNE  CMPS DEST,SOURCE
```

compares SOURCE to DEST, element by element, until 100 elements have been compared or until the 8086 finds an element in DEST that *matches* the corresponding element in SOURCE.

Move-String Instructions

Move String (MOVS)

MOVS copies a byte or word from one portion of memory to another. It has the general format

```
MOVS dest-string,source-string
```

where *source-string* is a string in the data segment and *dest-string* is a string in the extra segment. As with CMPS, the 8086 uses SI to address the data segment and DI to address the extra segment. So *MOVS copies one byte or word from the data segment to the extra segment.*

You may override the segment assignment for SI, but not for DI. For instance, you might override SI to copy a string from one part of the extra segment to another.

Athough MOVS moves only one element, you can move a string of up to 64K bytes (32K words) by applying the REP prefix. Example 3–4 shows a sequence that copies a 100-byte string called SOURCE in the data segment into the extra segment, where it is called DEST. As demonstrated here, every multi-element MOVS operation involves five steps:

1. Clear DF (with CLD) or set DF (with STD), depending on whether you want the move to progress toward higher addresses in memory or lower addresses in memory, respectively.
2. Load the offset of the source string into SI.
3. Load the offset of the destination string into DI.
4. Load the element count (number of bytes or words to be moved) into CX.
5. Execute the MOVS instruction, with a REP prefix.

Of course, your program must include an *extra segment* that holds space for the destination string and a *data segment* that holds the source string. Generally, you reserve space for the destination string with a directive such as

```
DEST DW 100 DUP(?)
```

Example 3–4. A Multi-Byte Move Operation

```
; This sequence copies 100 bytes from a string
; called SOURCE in the data segment to a string
; called DEST in the extra segment.
;
        CLD                     ;Set DF = 0, to move
                                ; forward
        LEA   SI,SOURCE         ;Load offset of SOURCE
                                ; into SI
        LEA   DI,ES:DEST        ; and offset of DEST
                                ; into DI
        MOV   CX,100            ;Load element count
                                ; into CX
REP  MOVS  DEST,SOURCE          ;Move the bytes
```

How does the assembler know whether you are moving bytes or words? It determines this based on the *type* of the source and destination labels in the operand field.

If these labels have the type attribute BYTE (that is, if they were set up with DB directives), the assembler encodes MOVS as a MOVSB instruction. Conversely, if the operand labels have the type attribute WORD (that is, if they were set up with DW directives), the assembler encodes MOVS as a MOVSW instruction. Therefore, if you define SOURCE and DEST with DW directives, the sequence in Example 3–4 copies 100 words instead of 100 bytes.

Move Byte String (MOVSB) and Move Word String (MOVSW)

Besides the fact that the MOVS instruction's operands remind you which strings are involved in the move, of what value are they? That is, what do they tell the assembler? They tell it simply to translate MOVS into one of the two forms the 8086 can execute: MOVSB (Move Byte String) or MOVSW (Move Word String). To make this translation, the assembler doesn't need to know *which* strings are affected (that information is in SI and DI), but only what size elements they have!

Since element size is the only thing the assember finds out from MOVS, there is no reason we can't use the size-specific instructions MOVSB and MOVSW instead of the general instruction MOVS. In fact, MOVSB and MOVSW are preferable to MOVS, because they save the assembler from looking up the size of the operands. As you might expect, these instructions have no operands; their forms are:

```
MOVSB
MOVSW
```

Thus, for example, we could write the instructions in Example 3–4 as follows:

```
        CLD
        LEA       SI,SOURCE
        LEA       DI,ES:DEST
        MOV       CX,100
REP     MOVSB
```

Overriding the Segment Assignments

Although SI normally addresses the data segment, you can use a different segment by applying a *segment override* prefix to the source operand. For example,

```
LEA       SI,ES:HERE
LEA       DI,ES:THERE
MOVSB
```

copies a byte from HERE to THERE, where both strings are in the extra segment.

Since you can't override DI, it appears the destination must always be a string in the extra segment. Does this mean you can't copy a string into the data segment? No, you *can* copy a string into the data segment, but it takes some trickery.

To copy a string into the data segment, you need to give the extra segment register (ES) the same value as the data segment register (DS). After that, when you execute MOVS, the 8086 will "think" it is copying a string from the data segment to the extra segment, as usual. But *you* know it is in fact copying a string from one place in the data segment to another!

Example 3–5 shows how this "trick" can be used to copy 100 bytes from SOURCE_D to DEST_D, where both strings are in the data segment. Note that except for the first two instructions, this sequence is identical to Example 3–4. You can also apply this technique to the other string instructions we discuss in this section.

Example 3–5. A Data Segment Move Operation

```
; This sequence copies 100 bytes from a string
; called SOURCE_D to a string called DEST_D,
; where both strings are in the data segment.
        MOV     SI,DS          ;Make ES point to data
        MOV     ES,SI          ; segment
        CLD                    ;Set DF = 0, to move
                               ; forward
        LEA     SI,SOURCE_D    ;Load offset of SOURCE_
                               ; D into SI
        LEA     DI,DEST_D      ; and offset of DEST_D
                               ; into DI
        MOV     CX,100         ;Load element count
                               ; into CX
REP     MOVSB                  ;Move the bytes
```

Compare-String Instructions

Compare Strings (CMPS)

Like the Compare (CMP) instruction we discussed in Section 3.5, the *Compare Strings (CMPS)* instruction compares a source operand to a destination operand, and returns the results in the flags. CMPS, like CMP, affects neither operand.

The general form of CMPS is

```
CMPS dest-string,source-string
```

where *source-string* is a string in the data segment addressed by SI and *dest-string* is a string in the extra segment addressed by DI. Therefore, CMPS compares an element (byte or word) in the data segment with an element in the extra segment.

Like the CMP instruction, CMPS compares the two operands by subtracting them. CMP, however, subtracts the source operand from the destination operand, whereas *CMPS subtracts the destination operand from the source operand!* This means the conditional transfer instructions that follow a CMPS instruction must be different than those that follow a CMP instruction. Table 3–13 is the one you need with CMPS.

To compare more than one element, you must apply a repeat prefix to the CMPS instruction. Here, REP would be meaningless, because it

Table 3–13. Using conditional transfers with CMPS.

| | *Follow CMP with* | |
| | *For Unsigned Numbers* | *For Signed Numbers* |
To Jump If		
Source is greater than Destination	JA	JG
Source is equal to Destination	JE	JE
Source is not equal to Destination	JNE	JNE
Source is less than Destination	JB	JL
Source is less than or equal to Destination	JBE	JLE
Source is greater than or equal to Destination	JAE	JGE

would return only the flags result of comparing the two final elements. You must prefix CMPS with either REPE (REPZ) or REPNE (REPNZ).

REPE makes the 8086 compare the strings until (CX) is zero or it finds two mismatched elements. Thus,

```
    CLD
    MOV   CX,100
REPE CMPS DEST,SOURCE
```

compares up to 100 elements of SOURCE and DEST in an attempt to find two elements that are unalike.

REPNE makes the 8086 compare the strings until (CX) is zero or it finds two identical elements. Thus,

```
      CLD
      MOV   CX,100
REPNE   CMPS DEST,SOURCE
```

compares up to 100 elements of SOURCE and DEST in an attempt to find two elements that are alike.

As with MOVS, the Direction Flag (DF) determines whether the operation proceeds forward (DF = 0) or backward (DF = 1) in memory, and SI and DI are updated after each operation.

Checking Results

Since repeated compare operations can terminate on either of two conditions—contents of CX are zero, or ZF changed to 0 (REPE) or 1 (REPNE)—you will want to determine which of these caused the termination. The easiest way to find out what stopped the compare is to follow CMPS with a conditional transfer instruction that tests ZF: either JE (JZ) or JNE (JNZ).

For example, the following sequence make the 8086 jump to NOT_FOUND if the first 100 elements of DEST and SOURCE do not match:

```
             CLD
             MOV   CX,100
REPNE        CMPS  DEST,SOURCE   ;Search for a
                                 ; match
             JNE   NOT_FOUND     ;Matching elements
             ..                  ; found?
             ..                  ; Yes. Continue
                                 ; here
NOT_FOUND:   ..                  ; No. Continue
                                 ; here

             ..
```

Compare Byte Strings (CMPSB) and
Compare Word Strings (CMPSW)

The assembler translates CMPS to either CMPSB (for bytes) or CMPSW (for words). You are encouraged to use these size-specific, no-operand forms instead of CMPS.

Scan-String Instructions

The scan-string instructions let you search a string in the extra segment for a specific value. The offset of the string's first element is in DI.

If you are scanning a byte string, the search value must be in AL. If you are scanning a word string, it must be in AX. The scan operation is nothing more than a compare-with-accumulator operation, and affects the flags in the same way as the string-compare instructions.

Scan String (SCAS)

The basic instruction in this group, *Scan String (SCAS)*, has the general form

```
SCAS dest-string
```

where *dest-string* identifies a string in the extra segment whose offset is in DI. This operand tells the 8086 whether the search value is a byte in AL or a word in AX.

As with CMPS, to operate on more than one string element, you should apply the repeat prefix REPE (REPZ) or REPNE (REPNZ). For example, this sequence

```
             CLD
             LEA   DI,ES:B_STRING
```

```
        MOV     AL,10
        MOV     CX,100
REPE    SCAS    B_STRING
```

searches up to 100 elements of the byte string *B_STRING*, trying to find an element that does not contain 10. If such an element is found, the offset of the *next* element is returned in DI and ZF is 0. A subsequent JCXZ instruction will tell you whether the element was found (jump not taken) or not found (jump taken).

Scan Byte String (SCASB) and Scan Word String (SCASW)

The assembler translates SCAS to either SCASB (for bytes) or SCASW (for words). You are encouraged to use these size-specific, no-operand forms instead of SCAS.

Load-String and Store-String Instructions

Once you have located a string element with a compare-string of scan-string instruction, you normally want to perform some operation on that element. You may want to read the element into a register (perhaps to determine its exact value) or change the element in memory. The load-string and store-string instructions provide these operations.

Load String (LODS)

The *Load String (LODS)* instruction transfers a *source-string* operand, addressed by SI, from the data segment to accumulator AL (byte operation) or AX (word operation), then adjusts SI to point to the next element. SI is incremented if DF is 0, and decremented if DF is 1.

For example, the following sequence compares the 500-byte strings DEST and SOURCE to find the first nonmatching elements. If a mismatch is detected, the SOURCE string element is loaded into AL.

```
        CLD
        LEA     DI,ES:DEST      ;Get offset of DEST
        LEA     SI,SOURCE       ; and SOURCE
        MOV     CX,500          ;Element count
REPE    CMPSB                   ;Search for a
                                ; mismatch
        JCXZ    MATCH           ;Mismatch found?
        DEC     SI              ; Yes. Adjust SI,
        LODS    SOURCE          ;   read element into
        ..                      ; AL, and process
        ..                      ;   it
```

```
MATCH:    ..                            ;No mismatch.
          ..                            ; Continue here
```

Because this is a byte operation, the element pointer (SI) is either in-cremented by 1 (if DF = 0) or decremented by 1 (if DF = 1) by the LODS instruction.

As usual, LODS has the optional shorter forms *Load Byte String (LODSB)* and *Load Word String (LODSW)*.

Store String (STOS)

The *Store String (STOS)* instruction transfers the value in AL (byte operation) or AX (word operation) to the *destination-string* operand in the extra segment, addressed by DI, then adjusts DI to point to the next element. DI is incremented if DF is 0, and decremented if DF is 1.

As a repeated operation, STOS is convenient for filling a string with a given value. For instance, the following sequence scans the 200-word string *W_STRING* for the first non-zero element. If such an element is found, this word and the next five words are filled with zeros.

```
            CLD
            LEA     DI,ES:W_STRING    ;Address string
            MOV     AX,0              ;Search value is
                                      ; 0
            MOV     CX,200            ;Search count is
                                      ; 200 words
   REPNE    SCASW                     ;Search the
                                      ; string
            JCXZ    ALLO              ;Nonzero word
                                      ; found?
            SUB     DI,2              ; Yes. Adjust DI,
            MOV     CX,6              ; then fill six
                                      ; words
   REP      STOS    W_STRING          ; with 0
   ALLOS:   ..                        ;No. Continue
                                      ; here

            ..
```

3.9 Interrupt Instructions

An interrupt is similar to a procedue call in that both make the 8086 save return information on the stack, then jump to an instruction se-quence elsewhere in memory. A procedure call makes the 8086 execute a procedure, while an interrupt makes it execute an *interrupt service routine*.

Although procedure calls can be NEAR or FAR and direct or indirect, an interrupt always makes an indirect jump to its service routine. It does this by taking the address of the routine from a 32-bit *interrupt vector* in memory. Moreover, procedure calls save only an address on the stack, whereas interrupts also save the flags on the stack (as a PUSHF instruction does).

Interrupts can be initiated by external devices in the system or by special interrupt instructions within a program. The 8086 has three different interrupt instructions—two "calls" and one "return"—as summarized in Table 3–14.

Interrupt (INT)

The INT instruction has the general form

```
INT interrupt-type
```

where *interrupt-type* is the identification number of one of 256 different vectors in memory.

When INT is executed, the 8086 does the following:

1. Pushes the Flags register onto the stack.
2. Clears the Trap Flag (TF) and the Interrupt Enable/Disable Flag (IF), to disable single-stepping and "lock out" other maskable interrupts.
3. Pushes the CS register onto the stack.
4. Calculates the address of the interrupt vector, by multiplying *interrupt-type* by 4.
5. Loads the second word of the interrupt vector into CS.
6. Pushes the IP onto the stack.
7. Loads the first word of the interrupt vector into IP.

In summary, after INT has executed, the flags CS and IP are on the stack, TF and IF are 0, and the CS:IP combination points to the starting address of the interrupt service routine. Now the 8086 begins executing the interrupt service routine.

The 256 interrupt vectors are located in the lowest locations in memory. Since each is 4 bytes long, they occupy a total of 1K bytes—absolute

Table 3–14. Interrupt instructions.

Mnemonic	Assembler Format		OF	DF	IF	TF	SF	ZF	AF	PF	CF
					Flags						
INT	INT	interrupt-type	—	—	0	0	—	—	—	—	—
INTO	INTO		—	—	0	0	—	—	—	—	—
IRET	IRET		*	*	*	*	*	*	*	*	*

Note: — means unchanged and * means changed.

addresses 0 trough 3FFH. For example, the instruction

```
INT 1AH
```

makes the 8086 calculate the vector address 68H (4 × 1AH), and fetch the 16-bit IP and CS values of the interrupt service routine from locations 68H and 6AH, respectively.

Figure 3–11 shows the stack, the Stack Pointer (SP), the Code Segment (CS) register, and the Instruction Pointer (IP) before and after this instruction is executed. In this example, the interrupt vector is assumed to hold the address F000:FE6E, so that is where the 8086 begins executing.

Of the 256 interrupt types, Intel has reserved the first five (Types 0 through 4) to internal interrupts in every 8086 or 8088 system. Various computers use some of the remaining interrupt types for their own internal functions and their disk operating systems.

Interrupt If Overflow (INTO)

The *Interrupt If Overflow (INTO)* instruction is a *conditional* INT instruction. INTO only activates an interrupt if the Overflow Flag (OF) is 1.

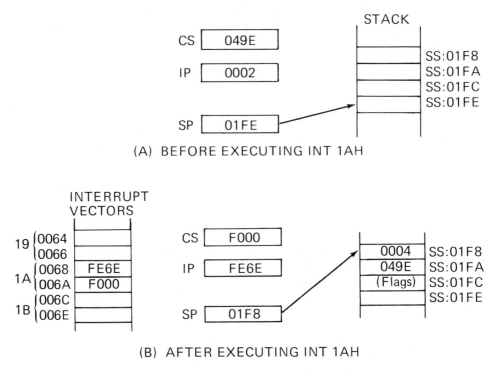

Figure 3–11. How an interrupt affects the stack.

In that case, INTO transfers control to an interrupt serice routine with an indirect call through interrupt vector 4. In other words, INTO activates a Type 4 interrupt.

Interrupt Return (IRET)

The *Interrupt Return (IRET)* instruction is to interrupts what RET is to procedure calls. It "undoes" the work of the original operation and lets the 8086 make an orderly return to the main program. For this reason, IRET must be the last instruction the 8086 executes in an interrupt service routine.

IRET pops three 16-bit values off the stack and loads them into the Instruction Pointer (IP), the Code Segment (CS) register, and the Flags register, respectively. Other program registers may be destroyed unless the interrupt service routine includes provisions to save them.

3.10 Processor Control Instructions

These instructions let you regulate the operation of the 8086 microprocessor from within a program. As Table 3–15 shows, there are three kinds of processor control instructions: flag operations, external synchronization, and the "do-nothing" instruction, NOP (no operation).

Table 3–15. Processor control instructions.

		Flags								
Mnemonic	*Assembler Format*	OF	DF	IF	TF	SF	ZF	AF	PF	CF
FLAG OPERATIONS										
STC	STC	—	—	—	—	—	—	—	—	1
CLC	CLC	—	—	—	—	—	—	—	—	0
CMC	CMC	—	—	—	—	—	—	—	—	*
STD	STD	—	1	—	—	—	—	—	—	—
CLD	CLD	—	0	—	—	—	—	—	—	—
STI	STI	—	—	1	—	—	—	—	—	—
CLI	CLI	—	—	0	—	—	—	—	—	—
EXTERNAL SYNCHRONIZATION										
HLT	HLT	—	—	—	—	—	—	—	—	—
WAIT	WAIT	—	—	—	—	—	—	—	—	—
ESC	ESC ext-opcode,source	—	—	—	—	—	—	—	—	—
LOCK	LOCK	—	—	—	—	—	—	—	—	—
NO OPERATION										
NOP	NOP	—	—	—	—	—	—	—	—	—

Note: — means unchanged and * means changed.

Flag Operations

The 8086 has seven instructions that let you change the Carry Flag (CF), Direction Flag (DF), and Interrupt Enable Flag (IF).

Set Carry Flag (STC) and *Clear Carry Flag (CLC)* force CF to a 1 or 0 state, respectively. These are useful to pre-condition CF for an RCL or RCR rotate-with-carry operation. *Complement Carry Flag (CMC)* makes CF a 0 if it is a 1, and vice versa.

Set Direction Flag (STD) and *Clear Direction Flag (CLD)* force DF to a 1 or 0 state, respectively. You use STD and CLD to select the direction for a string operation. If DF is 0, the index registers SI and DI increment after each operation. If DI is 1, they decrement after each operation. For example,

```
    MOV   CX,100
    CLD
REP MOVS DEST,SOURCE
```

moves elements SOURCE through SOURCE + 99 to the locations DEST through DEST + 99. Conversely,

```
    MOV   CX,100
    STD
REP MOVS DEST,SOURCE
```

moves elements SOURCE through SOURCE − 99 to the locations DEST through DEST − 99.

Clear Interrupt Flag (CLI) zeros IF, which makes the 8086 "ignore" maskable interrupts from external devices in the system. You disable such interrupts when the processor is performing some time-critical or high-priority task that cannot be interrupted. The processor will still process *nonmaskable* interrupts, however, while IF is 0.

Set Interrupt Flag (STI) sets IF to 1, which lets the 8086 respond to maskable interrupts from external devices.

External Synchronization Instructions

These instructions are used primarily to synchronize the 8086 microprocessor with external events.

Halt (HLT) puts the 8086 into a halt state. In this state, the processor sits idle and executes no instructions. The 8086 leaves the halt state only if you reset it or it receives an external interrupt, either nonmaskable or (if IF is 1) maskable. You may use HLT to make the processor wait for an interrupt before proceeding.

Wait (WAIT) also puts the 8086 into an idle state, but instead of just sitting there, it checks an input line called TEST at five-clock intervals.

(It will service interrupts during this time, however, but goes idle again upon return from the interrupt service routine.) If TEST is active, the 8086 proceeds to the instruction that follows WAIT. The purpose of WAIT is to stop the processor until some external device has completed its activity. For example, if the 8086 in your computer shares its data bus with an 8087 Numeric Data Processor (NDP), you may want to make the 8086 wait while the NDP is accessing memory. We discuss the 8087 in Chapter 7.

After reading how HLT and WAIT stop the processor, you might think that *Escape (ESC)* sends it on vacation! Not true. ESC simply makes it fetch the contents of a specified operand and put that operand on its data bus. Thus, ESC provides a way for other processors in the system to receive their instructions from the 8086 instruction stream.

The general form for ESC is

```
ESC ext-opcode,source
```

where *ext-opcode* is a 6-bit immediate number and *source* is a register or a memory variable. For example, if you have an 8087 NDP in the system, you can send it instructions with ESCs. Here, the NDP's op-code is *ext-opcode* and its operand is the contents of *source*.

Lock the Bus (LOCK) is a 1-byte prefix that may precede any instruction. LOCK makes the 8086 activate its bus LOCK signal for as long as the LOCKed instruction takes to execute. While the LOCK signal is active, no other processor in the system can use the bus.

No Operation Instruction

The final instruction, *No Operation (NOP)*, is the simplest of all, because it does exactly what its name implies—it performs no operation whatsoever. It affects no flags, no registers, and no memory locations. It only advances the Instruction Pointer (IP).

What good is NOP? Surprisingly, NOP has a variety of uses. For example, you can use its op-code (90H) to "patch" object code when you want to delete an instruction without re-assembling the program. NOP is also convenient when you are testing sequences of instructions in your computer. That is, you can make NOP the last instruction in a test program—a convenient spot at which to stop a trace. You may find other uses for this innocuous, but handy, instruction.

Exercises (answers on page 206)

1. Write an instruction that stores the contents of the AX register into a word location called SAVE_AX in the extra segment.

2. What does this sequence do?

```
MOV AX,0
MOV BX,AX
MOV BP,AX
MOV [BX],AX
MOV [BP],AX
```

3. Which of the following instructions or sequences are invalid? (Assume variables are defined in the data segment and instructions are defined in the code segment.)

```
(a)  K      EQU 1024
            . .
            . .
            MOV K,AX
(b)  TEMP   DB   ?
            . .
            . .
            MOV AL,TEMP
(c)  TEMP   DB   ?
            . .
            . .
            MOV TEMP,AX
(d)  TEMP   DB   ?
     T3     DB 10
            . .
            . .
            MOV TEMP,T3
(e)         MOV [BX][BP],AX
```

4. List two instructions that clear the AX register to zero.
5. How do these two instructions differ?

```
MOV BX,OFFSET TABLE+4
LEA BX,TABLE+4
```

6. Write a loop that subtracts a three-word variable called V2 from another three-word variable called V1.
7. What does this instruction do?

```
MUL 10
```

8. If AX contains 1234H and BX contains 4321H, list the contents of AX after each of these instructions is executed:

```
(a)    AND    AX,BX
(b)    OR     AX,BX
(c)    XOR    AX,BX
(d)    NOT    AX
(e)    TEST   AX,BX
```

9. Write a sequence to *normalize* AX. That is, shift AX left until the most-sigificant "1" bit is in Bit 15. If AX is initially zero or Bit 15 already contains a 1, exit immediately.
10. What does this sequence do?

```
START:     MOV     CX,3
           SUB     AX,10
           LOOP    START
```

4

High-Precision Mathematics

If you have done any assembly language programming on one of the conventional microprocessors, you are probably impressed with the arithmetic potential of the 8086. For starters, the very fact that the 8086 has built-in multiply and divide instructions means the hours (or days) of time you normally spend developing multiplication and division programs are available for more stimulating activities, such as playing racquetball.

In this chapter we build on the potential offered by the multiply and divide instructions to develop some programs that tackle tougher math problems. We will begin with programs that multiply 32-bit signed and unsigned numbers. From these, we will discuss how to handle overflow situations in divide operations, and conclude with a program that calculates square roots.

4.1 Multiplication

In Chapter 3 we studied the 8086's two multiplication instructions, *Multiply, Unsigned (MUL)* and *Integer Multiply, Signed (IMUL)*. These instructions multiply byte- or word-length operands to produce double-length (16- or 32-bit) products.

Is it difficult to multiply numbers larger than 16 bits? No, it's not difficult at all, as you shall see. Anyone who has written a multiplication program for an earlier 8-bit microprocessor knows that just *having* a multiply instruction of any kind makes up for whatever inconvenience you go through to extend its capabilities.

Unsigned 32-Bit × 32-Bit Multiply

Although the MUL instruction can handle only 8- or 16-bit operands, you can use it to multiply multiprecision unsigned numbers. For instance, you can use MUL to multiply two 32-bit numbers. To do this, you calculate a series of 32-bit *cross products,* then combine them to form the final 64-bit product. You learned this method in elementary school to multiply decimal numbers with pencil and paper.

As you probably recall (in these days of pocket calculators, it may be a little hazy), you write the multiplicand with the multiplier below it and perform a series of multiplications—one for each digit in the multiplier. Each individual multiplication produces a partial product, which you enter directly below the multiplier digit. Thus, each partial product is offset one digit position to the left of the preceding partial product.

For example, 124 times 103 looks like this:

```
     124 Multiplicand
  × 103 Multiplier
     372 Partial Product #1
     000   Partial Product #2
     124   Partial Product #3
   12772 Final Product
```

Offsetting the partial products accounts for the *decimal weights* of the multiplier digits. In this example, the 3 is a "ones" digit, the 0 is a "tens" digit, and the 1 is a "hundreds" digit. Therefore, you could write the example as:

$$103 \times 124 = (3 \times 124) + (0 \times 124) + (100 \times 124)$$

or

$$103 \times 124 = (3 \times 1 \times 124) + (0 \times 10 \times 124) + (1 \times 100 \times 124)$$

In this section we will develop a short procedure that multiplies two 32-bit unsigned numbers and yields a 64-bit unsigned product. If you had no multiply instruction you would have to perform 32 separate multiplications, one for each bit in the multiplier.

But fortunately the 8086 has an instruction that multiplies 16-bit unsigned numbers directly. This instruction, MUL, lets us regard a 32-bit multiplier and a 32-bit multiplicand as two 2-digit numbers, where each digit is 16 bits long. Thus, we can generate the 64-bit product with just *four* multiplications.

Figure 4–1 shows a symbolic representation of the multiplier (digits A and B) and the multiplicand (digits C and D), and illustrates how the four partial products are derived and how they must be aligned to

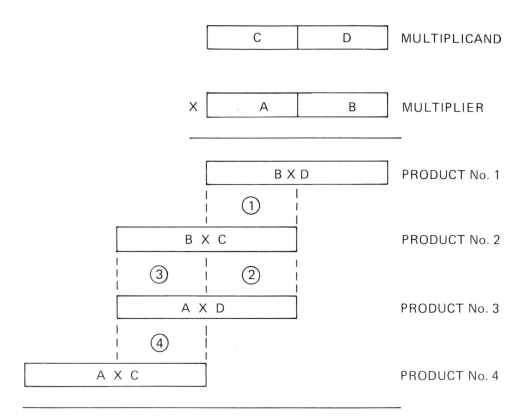

TOTAL = 64 – BIT FINAL PRODUCT

Figure 4–1. Generating a 64-bit product with four 16-bit by 16-bit multiplications.

calculate the 64-bit final product. The circled numbers in Figure 4–1 identify the four 16-bit additions you must make to calculate the final product. (For instance, Addition 1 adds the high 16 bits of Product #1 to the low 16 bits of Product #2.)

Using Figure 4–1 as a guide, we can develop a procedure that multiplies two 32-bit numbers. Example 4–1 shows such a procedure, labeled MULU32, where the multiplier and multiplicand are entered in register pairs CX:BX and DX:AX, respectively. The 64-bit unsigned product is returned in these same four registers: DX (high 16 bits), CX (mid-upper 16 bits), BX (mid-lower 16 bits), and AX (low 16 bits). Example 4–1 also shows some scratch locations that you must set up in the data segment.

The MULU32 procedure is fairly straightforward if you refer to Figure 4–1 as you look at the instructions and their accompanying comments. MULU32 begins by saving the multiplicand in memory, then generating the four 32-bit partial products. Once the partial products have been saved in memory, the only remaining step is to add them. Note that the Carry Flag stays intact between additions because MOV does not affect CF.

Example 4-1. A 32-Bit × 32-Bit Unsigned Multiply Procedure

```
; This procedure multiplies two 32-bit unsigned
; numbers and generates a 64-bit product. Enter
; with the multiplier in CX (high word) and BX
; (low word) and the multiplicand in DX (high
; word) and AX (low word). The product is
; returned in DX, CX, BX, and AX (high to low
; order).
;
; Set up these variables in the data segment:
;
HI_MCND   DW  ?
LO_MCND   DW  ?
HI_PP1    DW  ?
LO_PP1    DW  ?
HI_PP2    DW  ?
LO_PP2    DW  ?
HI_PP3    DW  ?
LO_PP3    DW  ?
HI_PP4    DW  ?
LO_PP4    DW  ?
;
; The main procedure follows.
;
MULU32 PROC
        MOV   HI_MCND,DX    ;Save multiplicand in
        MOV   LO_MCND,AX    ; memory
        MUL   BX            ;Form partial product
                           ; #1
        MOV   HI_PP1,DX     ; and save it in memory
        MOV   LO_PP1,AX
        MOV   AX,HI_MCND    ;Form partial product
                           ; #2
        MUL   BX
        MOV   HI_PP2,DX     ; and save it in memory
        MOV   LO_PP2,AX
        MOV   AX,LO_MCND    ;Form partial product
                           ; #3
        MUL   CX
        MOV   HI_PP3,DX     ; and save it in memory
        MOV   LO_PP3,AX
        MOV   AX,HI_MCND    ;Form partial product
                           ; #4
        MUL   CX
        MOV   HI_PP4,DX     ; and save it in memory
        MOV   LO_PP4,AX
;
; Add the partial products to form the 64-bit
; final product.
;
        MOV   AX,LO_PP1     ;Low 16 bits
```

```
          MOV  BX,HI_PP1    ;Form mid-lower 16 bits
          ADD  BX,LO_PP2    ; with sum #1
          ADC  HI_PP2,0
          ADD  BX,LO_PP3    ; and sum #2
          MOV  CX,HI_PP2    ;Form mid-upper 16 bits
          ADC  CX,HI_PP3    ; with sum #3
          ADC  HI_PP4,0
          ADD  CX,LO_PP4    ; and sum #4
          MOV  DX,HI_PP4    ;Form high 16 bits
          ADC  DX,0         ; with propagated carry
          RET
   MULU32 ENDP
```

Since a 32-bit operand can represent unsigned values as large as 4.294 $\times$ 10^9, the MULU32 procedure is satisfactory for most applications. (For those that involve larger numbers, you will probably use floating-point math!) It is certainly possible, however, to develop a procedure that multiplies 64-bit (or longer) numbers with the cross-products approach used in Example 4–1.

Signed 32-Bit $\times$ 32-Bit Multiply

Although we described Example 4–1 as a procedure to multiply two unsigned numbers, it can also multiply two signed numbers, as long as both numbers are positive. In other words, Example 4–1 provides a 32-bit $\times$ 32-bit "non-negative" multiply procedure. This procedure cannot properly multiply negative numbers because such numbers are represented in *twos-complement* form.

What happens if we simply replace each MUL instruction in Example 4–1 with an IMUL (Integer Multiply, Signed) instruction? That won't do the job either because IMUL assumes that the most-significant bit of each operand is a sign indicator, which is not the case when we generate cross products.

How, then, can we multiply 32-bit signed numbers? One way is to negate the negative operand(s), perform a normal unsigned multiplication, then adjust the product, if required. If just one of the operands is negative, you must twos-complement the product. If both operands are negative, the (positive) product is correct as it stands.

We employ this simple approach in Example 4–2. There, a byte variable called NEG_IND holds a "negative indicator." This indicator is initially set to zero, and stays that way if both operands are positive. If one of the operands is negative, we take the ones-complement of NEG_IND, which makes it all ones. If both operands are negative, we ones-complement NEG_IND *twice*, which returns it to the all-zeros state.

Each time NEG_IND is ones-complemented, one of the operands is negated (twos-complemented). Because the 8086's NEG instruction operates only on byte or word operands, we must twos-complement our

32-bit operands in "brute-force" fashion. To do this, we ones-complement the operand, then add 1.

The MULS32 procedure calls MULU32 to perform the 32-bit by 32-bit multiplication. Since MULU32 is in another assembly module, we must declare it EXTRN at the start of the example. (Remember, the MULU32 module must have a PUBLIC MULU32 statement.) Upon return from MULU32, the state of NEG_IND determines whether the product is correct (NEG_IND zero) or needs negating (NEG_IND nonzero).

The execution times of the MUL32 procedure depends on whether the operands are both positive, both negative, or of opposite sign. Following is a summary of these execution times for the 8086, in both clock cycles and microseconds (with a 5-MHz clock). An 8088 would take 114 additional cycles.

Operands	Maximum Time (Cycles)	Maximum Time (μs)
Both positive	983	196.6
Opposite signs	1,023	204.6
Both negative	1,032	206.4

Example 4–2. A 32-Bit × 32-Bit Signed Multiply Procedure

```
; This procedure multiplies two 32-bit signed
; numbers and generates a 64-bit product. Enter
; with the multiplier in CX (high word) and BX
; (low word) and the multiplicand in DX (high
; word) and AX (low word). The product is
; returned in DX, CX, BX, and AX (high to low
; order).
; This procedure calls MULU32 (Example 4-1).
;
; Set up this variable, and those listed in
; Example 4-1, in the data segment.
;
NEG_IND DB ?
;
; The main procedure follows.
;
EXTRN   MULU32: FAR          ;MULU32 is an external
                             ; procedure
MULS32 PROC
       MOV     NEG_IND,0     ;Negative indicator = 0
       CMP     DX,0          ;Multiplicand negative?
       JNS     CHKCX         ; No. Check multiplier
       NOT     AX            ; Yes. Twos-complement
       NOT     DX            ; multiplicand
       ADD     AX,1
       ADC     DX,0
```

```
                NOT     NEG_IND     ; and ones-complement
                                    ; indicator
        CHKCX:  CMF     CX,0        ;Multiplier negative?
                JNS     GOMUL       ; No. Multiply
                NOT     BX          ; Yes. Twos-complement
                NOT     CX          ; multiplier
                ADD     BX,1
                ADC     CX,0
                NOT     NEG_IND     ; and ones-complement
                                    ; indicator
        GOMUL:  CALL    MULU32      ;Perform unsigned
                                    ; multiplication
                CMP     NEG_IND,0   ;Does product have
                                    ; correct sign?
                JZ      DONE        ; Yes. Exit
                NOT     AX          ; No. Twos-complement
                NOT     BX          ;  product
                NOT     BX
                NOT     CX
                NOT     DX
                ADD     AX,1
                ADC     BX,0
                ADC     CX,0
                ADC     DX,0
        DONE:   RET
        MUL32   ENDP
```

4.2 Division

There are many applications for division, but one of the most common is taking the average of a set of numbers—perhaps the results of a series of laboratory tests. Example 4–3 shows a typical averaging program.

This procedure, AVERAGE, averages a specified number of unsigned word values pointed to by BX; the word count is contained in CX. It returns the integer portion of the average in AX and the fractional remainder in DX. For example, you could use this sequence to average a 100-word table called TABLE:

```
LEA   BX,TABLE   ;Fetch offset of TABLE
MOV   CX,100     ; and its word count
CALL  AVERAGE    ;Calculate the average
```

Example 4–3. A Word-Averaging Procedure

```
; This procedure takes the average of a
; specified number of unsigned word values in
; the data segment. The offset of the first word
; is contained in BX and the word count is
```

```
; contained in CX.
; Upon return, the integer portion of the
; average is in AX and the fractional remainder
; is in DX.
;
AVERAGE  PROC
         SUB   AX,AX      ;Clear dividend to start
         SUB   DX,DX
         PUSH  CX         ;Save word count on stack
ADD_W:   ADD   AX,[BX]    ;Add next word to total
         ADC   DX,0
         ADD   BX,2       ; and update the index
         LOOP  ADD_W      ;All words now totaled?
         POP   CX         ; Yes. Retrieve word count
         DIV   CX         ;  and take the average
         RET
AVERAGE  ENDP
```

In describing the DIV and IDIV instructions (Section 3.5), we mentioned that a divide operation automatically aborts if the divisor is zero or if an *overflow* condition exists. An overflow occurs when the dividend is so much larger than the divisor that the result register can't hold the quotient. An unsigned division overflows if the dividend is more than 65,535 times greater than the divisor.

Both divide-by-zero and overflow make the 8086 activate a Type 0 (Divide by Zero) interrupt. In most computers, this interrupt saves the register contents, displays a message (perhaps *Divide Overflow*), then terminates the program.

Naturally, the divide operation in Example 4–3 aborts if CX holds zero upon entry. Can an overflow also cause it to abort? No, overflow cannot occur here because the ratio of the dividend (word total) to the divisor (word count) can never exceed 65,536! However, some divide operations (for example, dividing 200,000 by 2) may produce an overflow. For this reason, it is worthwhile to look at a procedure that always gives a valid quotient, irrespective of overflow.

How to Deal with Overflow

In some applications, overflow signifies an error. In others, overflow is acceptable, but means that the program must be able to accommodate a quotient longer than 16 bits. Since the division aborts when the 8086 encounters an overflow condition, how can you obtain a longer quotient? One easy way to get this quotient is to split the 32-bit dividend into two 16-bit numbers, then perform two 16-bit by 16-bit divide operations (which cannot produce an overflow).

If the divisor is a 16-bit number called X and the dividend is a 32-bit number represented by Y_1Y_0, you can represent the divide operation as

$$X \overline{\smash{\big)}\, Y_1Y_0}$$

or, more properly, as

$$X \overline{\smash{\big)}\, (Y_1 \times 2^{16}) + Y_0}$$

This division produces two 16-bit quotient digits (Q_1 and Q_0) and two 16-bit remainder digits (R_1 and R_0), as follows:

$$X \overline{\smash{\big)}\, \overset{Q_1 \times 2^{16}}{Y_1 + 2^{16}}} \text{ and } R_1 \times 2^{16}$$

$$X \overline{\smash{\big)}\, \overset{Q_0}{(R_1 \times 2^{16}) + Y_0}} \text{ and } R_0$$

As you see, the combination of these two operations produce a 32-bit quotient, Q_1Q_0, and a 16-bit remainder, R_0. (The interim remainder R_1, if there is one, disappears during the second divide operation.) If no overflow occurs, Q_1 is zero, and the result is returned as $0Q_0$ and R_0.

With this approach we can develop a divide procedure that *always* returns a valid quotient and remainder, regardless of overflow. Example 4–4 gives a procedure called DIVUO that does the job. This procedure divides a 32-bit dividend in DX (high word) and AX (low word) by a 16-bit divisor in BX, and produces a 32-bit quotient in BX:AX and a 16-bit remainder in DX.

The DIVUO procedure is comprised of four steps:

1. Check whether the divisor in BX is zero. If so, call the Type 0 interrupt to abort the operation.
2. Change the Type 0 interrupt vector in absolute locations 0 (offset) and 2 (segment) so that it points to a new interrupt service routine—the one labeled OVER_INT in Example 4–4.
3. Perform the division. In the absence of overflow, the 8086 continues to the next consecutive instruction (SUB BX,BX). If overflow occurs, it activates the Type 0 interrupt service routine, which is now OVR_INT.
4. Restore the original Type 0 interrupt vector from values placed on the stack.

With or without overflow, the DIVUO procedure returns a 32-bit quotient (BX:AX) and a 16-bit remainder (DX). If no overflow occurs, BX is zero.

Example 4-4. A Division Procedure That Accounts for Overflow

```
; This divide procedure determines the correct
; quotient and remainder, regardless of overflow.
; Enter with the 16-bit divisor in BX and the 32-
; bit dividend in DX (high word) and AX (low
; word).
; The 32-bit quotient is returned in BX:AX and
; the 16-bit remainder is returned in DX.
;
DIVUO     PROC
          CMP    BX,0          ;Divisor = 0?
          JNZ    DVROK
          INT    0             ; Yes. Abort the
                               ;  divide
DVROK:    PUSH   ES            ; Save current ES
                               ;  register,
          PUSH   DI            ; DI register,
          PUSH   CX            ; and CX register
          MOV    DI,0          ;Fetch current INT 0
          MOV    ES,DI         ;  vector
          PUSH   ES:[DI]       ; and save it on the
          PUSH   ES:[DI+2]     ;  stack
          LEA    CX,OVR_INT    ;Make INT 0 vector
          MOV    ES:[DI],CX    ;  point to OVR_INT
          MOV    CX,SEG
                 OVR_INT
          MOV    ES:[DI+2],
                 CX
          DIV    BX            ;Perform the division
          SUB    BX,BX         ;If no overflow, make
                               ;  BX zero
RESTORE:  POP    ES:[DI+2]     ;Restore INT 0 vector
          POP    ES:[DI]
          POP    CX            ;Restore original CX,
          POP    DI            ;  DI,
          POP    ES            ;  and ES
          RET
;
; This interrupt routine is executed if the
; divide operation produces overflow.
;
OVER_INT: POP    CX            ;Modify return
                               ;  address offset
          LEA    CX,RESTORE    ;  to skip SUB BX,BX
          PUSH   CX
          PUSH   AX            ;Save current AX
                               ;  register
          MOV    AX,DX         ;Set up first
          SUB    DX,DX         ;  dividend, 0-Y1
```

```
          DIV    BX          ;Q1 is in AX, R1 is
                             ; in DX
          POP    CX          ;Fetch original AX
                             ; into CX
          PUSH   AX          ;Save Q1 on the stack
          MOV    AX,CX       ;Set up second
                             ; dividend, R1-Y0
          DIV    BX          ;Q0 is in AX, R0 is
                             ; in DX
          POP    BX          ;Final quotient is in
          IRET               ; BX:AX
DIVUO     ENDP
```

4.3 Square Root

In this final section we will develop a program to calculate the integer square root of a 32-bit unsigned number, using the classical method of successive approximations (also known as Newton's method). This method says that *if A is an approximation for the square root of a number N, then*

$$A1 = (N/A + A)/2$$

is a better approximation.

To illustrate, suppose you want to find the square root of a number that has the value N. To get the first approximation, use the formula $(N/200) + 2$. To get the second approximation, divide N by the first approximation, then average the two results. To get the third approximation, divide N by the second approximation and average, and so on. For example, to find the square root of 10,000:

N = 1,000; first approximation is (10,000/200) + 2, or 52
    10,000/52 = 192, (192 + 52)/2 = 122
    10,000/122 = 81, (122 + 81)/2 = 101
    10,000/101 = 99, (101 + 99)/2 = 100
    10,000/100 = 100

So the square root of 10,000 is 100. We know that 100 *is* the square root, rather than just another intermediate approximation, because 100 times 100 is 10,000.

This particular number, 10,000, happens to have an integer square root, but not many numbers do. For example, the square root of 9,999 is not an integer. This means if we try to computerize the successive approximation method and use

```
root x root = number
```

as the "all done" criteria, the processor will repeat the approximation instructions indefinitely, because the square of the *integer* approximation will never be 9,999. Surely there must be a better way to stop the processor once it has found the closest, or "best," square root for a number.

You can use several different methods to end the approximation procedure. The one that best suits your needs depends on how accurate your answer must be, and how much execution time you are willing to invest to get that answer.

For instance, you can let the 8086 execute the loop 10 times, and assume that answer is accurate enough. Although it satisfies many applications, this method is rather arbitrary. For a more precise solution, you can let the 8086 repeat the loop until it finds two successive approximations that are identical, or until they differ only by one. We take the latter approach in our software example.

Example 4–5 gives a procedure (SQRT32) that calculates the integer square root of a 32-bit number by successive approximations. In this procedure, the source number is contained in DX (high word) and AX (low word), and the 16-bit square root is returned in BX.

Example 4–5. Square Root of a 32-Bit Number

```
; This procedure calculates the square root of a
; 32-bit integer in DX (high word) and AX (low
; word), and returns that square root as a 16-bit
; integer in BX. The original number in DX:AX is
; not affected.
;
SQRT32      PROC
            PUSH  BP          ;Save contents of BP
            PUSH  DX          ; and source number
            PUSH  AX          ; DX:AX
            MOV   BP,SP        ;BP points to AX on
                              ; the stack
            MOV   BX,200       ;As a first
                              ; approximation,
            DIV   BX          ; divide source number
                              ; by 200,
            ADD   AX,2         ; then add 2
NXT_APP:    MOV   BX,AX        ;Save this
                              ; approximation in BX
            MOV   AX,[BP]      ;Read source number
            MOV   DX,[BP+2]    ; again
            DIV   BX          ;Divide it by last
                              ; approximation
            ADD   AX,BX        ;Average the last two
            SHR   AX,1         ; results
            CMP   AX,BX        ;Last two
                              ; approximations
                              ; identical?
```

```
                JE      DONE
                SUB     BX,AX        ; No. Check for
                CMP     BX,1         ; difference of 1
                JE      DONE
                CMP     BX,-1
                JNE     NXT_APP
    DONE:       MOV     BX,AX        ;Put result in BX
                POP     AX           ;Restore source number
                POP     DX
                POP     BP           ; and scratch register
                RET                  ;  BP
    SQRT32      ENDP
```

To begin, the procedure saves BP (which it uses as a stack pointer), DX, and AX on the stack, then copies the Stack Pointer (SP) into BP, so that BP points to AX on the stack. The first approximation is then derived using the formula (N/200) + 2. The instruction at NXT_APP is the beginning of a loop that extends to the label DONE.

Each time it passes through this loop, the 8086 calculates a new approximation by dividing the 32-bit source number (read from the stack) by the preceding approximation, then averaging these two results. It averages results with a right-shift operation, which effectively divides AX by 2. Using SHR instead of DIV here saves quite a bit of execution time—2 cycles for SHR versus a minimum of *80* cycles for DIV!

The procedure checks each new approximation against the preceding one, looking for approximations that are identical or differ by only 1 (+1 or −1). When any of these three conditions occur, the processor transfers to DONE; otherwise, it goes back to NXT_APP to calculate a new approximation. At DONE, the 8086 puts the final square-root value in BX, then pops the source number (AX and DX) and the original value of BP off the stack.

Exercise (answer on page 207)

1. An interesting observation made a few years ago gives us a simple way to calculate square roots. The observation is this: *The square root of an integer is equal to the number of successively higher odd numbers that can be subtracted from it.*

   Figure 4–2 shows how you can extract the square root of 25 using this method. (Skeptics will want to try a few additional cases.) In this example, a total of five odd numbers—1, 3, 5, 7, and 9—can be subtracted from 25, so the square root is 5.

   Develop a procedure that employs this algorithm to take the square root of the 32-bit unsigned number in DX (high word) and AX (low word), and returns the 16-bit square root in BX. As with Example 4–5, AX and DX should be returned intact.

```
   25
 - _1  Partial square root  = 1
   24
 - _3  Partial square root  = 2
   21
 - _5  Partial square root  = 3
   16
 - _7  Partial square root  = 4
    9
 - _9  Square root           = 5
    0
```

Figure 4–2. Obtaining a square root with odd-number subtractions.

5

Operating on Data Structures

There are almost as many ways to organize information in memory as there are kinds of information to be organized. These organizational techniques vary with the application, and have such names as lists, arrays, strings, and look-up tables. All of these are different kinds of *data structures*.

The subject of data structures can (and does) fill many volumes, so we can't hope to give it an exhaustive treatment in a book like this. Instead, we will concentrate on just three basic structures: *lists, look-up tables*, and *text files*.

Lists hold units of data (one or more bytes or words), called *elements*, arranged sequentially in memory. The sequence can be *consecutive*, where elements occupy adjacent memory locations, or *linked*, where each element includes a "pointer" to the next element in the list. Moreover, the elements may be randomly arranged or in ascending or descending order.

Look-up tables are data structures that hold information (either data or addresses) that has a defined relationship to a known value. A telephone directory is a look-up table; knowing a name, you can look up an associated telephone number.

Text files consist of non-numeric information such as letters, reports, telephone lists, and other similar files.

5.1 Unordered Lists

In our ordered society, where telephone book listings are arranged alphabetically and house numbers increase or decrease as you go up or down a street, unordered *anythings* somehow seem bothersome. Still, not everything can be neatly ordered, so unordered lists remain a fact of life in many applications, particularly those that involve random data or data that changes with time. For example, computerized weather stations may store hourly temperature readings in unordered lists and manufacturers may log monthly shipping statistics in unordered lists.

Most lists are composed of an element count byte (or word) and one or more data elements. When you work with a list, you generally want to add or delete elements, or search for an element of a certain value. These operations are fairly easy to do.

1. To add an element, you simply store it at the end of the list and add 1 to the element count.
2. To delete an element, you just move the remainder of the list (all elements following the one to be deleted) upward in memory, then subtract 1 from the element count.
3. To search for an element value, you compare each element to the search value, starting with the first element in the list.

Adding an Element to an Unordered List

Procedure ADD_TO_UL, shown in Example 5–1, is the kind of program you would use to create an unordered list or add an element to an existing unordered list. In this case, the list contains word values (either signed or unsigned).

ADD_TO_UL starts by reading the element count into CX, then scanning the data elements for the value in AX. If this value is already in the list (the final value of ZF is 0), the 8086 pops the starting address back into DI and returns. Otherwise, it adds the value to the end of this list and increases the element count by one.

How long does this procedure take to execute? That depends on the number of elements and whether the search value is already in the list. The primary factor is how many times the Scan String (SCASW) instruction is repeated. SCASW executes in (9 + 15N) cycles, where N is the number of repetitions. Let's examine the timing for both cases—value is not in the list and value is in the list—for a list that has N data elements.

If the search value is not in the list, the SCASW instruction executes N times. The remaining instructions in the procedure execute only once, and take 89 cycles. Therefore,

$$\text{Execution time} = 9 + 19N + 89$$
$$= 19N + 98 \text{ cycles}$$

Thus, adding an element to a 100-element list takes 1,998 cycles, or 399.6 μs at 5 MHz.

Example 5–1. Adding an Element to an Unordered List

```
; This procedure adds the value in AX to an
; unordered list in the extra segment, if that
; value is not already in the list. The starting
; address of the list is in DI. The length of the
; list, in words, is in the list's first
; location. DI and AX are returned unaltered.
;
ADD_TO_UL   PROC
            CLD                         ;Make DF = 0, to
                                        ; scan forward
            PUSH    DI                  ;Save starting
                                        ; address
            MOV     CX,ES:[DI]          ;Fetch word count
            ADD     DI,2                ;Make DI point to
                                        ; first data element
REPNE       SCASW                       ;Value already in the
                                        ; list?
            JNE     ADD_IT
            POP     DI                  ; Yes. Restore
                                        ;   starting address
            RET                         ;   and exit
ADD_IT:     STOSW                       ; No. Add it to end
                                        ; of
            POP     DI                  ; list, then update
                                        ; element count
            INC     WORD PTR ES: [DI]
            RET
ADD_TO_UL   ENDP
```

If the search value is in the list, it should take the 8086 an average of N/2 comparisons to locate it, because 50 percent of the time a search value will lie in the lower half of the list and 50 percent of the time it will lie in the upper half. This means the scan should theoretically take (9 + 7.5N) cycles. The remaining instructions in the procedure take an additional 44 cycles. Therefore, on the average,

$$\text{Execution time} = 9 + 7.5N + 44$$
$$= 7.5N + 53 \text{ cycles}$$

Thus, finding an element in an unordered 100-element list takes an average of 803 cycles, or 160.6 μs.

Deleting an Element from an Unordered List

To delete an element from an unordered list, you must find it, then move the rest of the elements up one position. In doing this, you write over the deletion "victim." Since an element has been removed, you decrease the element count (the first location in the list) by one.

To illustrate, Figure 5–1A shows a list of bytes in memory. This list has six data elements, so the first location (LIST) holds the value 6.

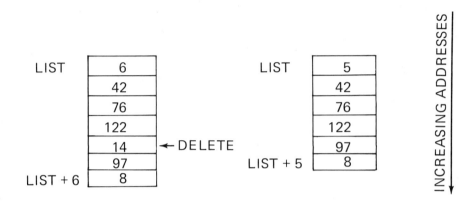

(A) BEFORE DELETION   (B) AFTER DELETION

Figure 5–1. How a deletion affects a list.

Figure 5–1B shows what the list looks like after the fourth element (the value 14) has been deleted. After the deletion, the list has only five data elements and the values 97 and 8 have moved up in memory, eradicating the deleted value.

The DEL_UL procedure in Example 5–2 performs just such an operation, using AX to specify the value to be deleted. As in Example 5–1, DI points to the start of the list.

The instructions that precede REPNE load the element count into CX and the address of the first element into DI, then scan the list for the search value. These instructions are identical to those at the beginning of Example 5–1. If the search value is in the list (ZF = 1), the 8086 jumps to DELETE.

At DELETE, the processor takes one of two paths. If the element to be deleted is at the end of the list (CX contains zero), the 8086 jumps to DEC_CNT, where it simply decreases the list's element count. If the element to be deleted is anywhere else in the list, the loop at NEXT_EL moves all remaining elements up one position, overwriting the deletion victim. The element count is then decreased by one to reflect the deletion.

Finding Maximum and Minimum Values in an Unordered List

In working with a list of unordered data, you often want to find the largest and smallest values in the list. One way to find them is to initially declare the first element as both the maximum and the minimum value, then compare each of the remaining elements in the list to those values. If your program finds an element whose value is less than the minimum, you make that value the new *minimum*. Similarly, if it finds an element whose value is greater than the maximum, you make that value the new *maximum*.

Example 5-2. Deleting an Element from an Unordered List

```
; This procedure deletes the value in AX from an
; unordered list in the extra segment, if that
; value is in the list. The starting address of
; the list is in DI. The length of the list, in
; words, is in the list's first location. DI and
; AX are returned unaltered.
;
DEL_UL    PROC
          CLD                        ;Make DF = 0, to scan
                                     ; forward
          PUSH    BX                 ;Save scratch
                                     ; register BX
          PUSH    DI                 ; and starting
                                     ; address
          MOV     CX,ES:[DI]         ;Fetch element count
          ADD     DI,2
REPNE     SCASW                      ;Value in the list?
          JE      DELETE             ; If so, delete it
          POP     DI                 ; Otherwise, restore
                                     ; registers
          POP     BX
          RET                        ; and exit
; The following instructions delete an element
; from the list, as follows:
;   (1)  If the element lies at the end of the
;        list, delete it by decreasing the element
;        count by 1.
;   (2)  Otherwise, delete the element by moving
;        all subsequent elements up by one
;        position.
;
DELETE:   JCXZ    DEC_CNT            ;If (CX) = 0,
                                     ; delete last
                                     ; element
NEXT_EL:  MOV     BX,ES:[DI]         ;Move one
          MOV     ES:[DI-2],BX       ; element up in
                                     ; list
          ADD     DI,2               ;Point to next
                                     ; element
          LOOP    NEXT_EL            ;Repeat until
                                     ; all are moved
DEC_CNT:  POP     DI                 ;Decrease
                                     ; element count
                                     ; by 1
          DEC     WORD PTR ES:[DI]
          POP     BX                 ;Restore BX
          RET                        ; and exit
DEL_UL    ENDP
```

The procedure MINMAX in Example 5–3 applies this method to an unordered list of unsigned word values. When you call this procedure, the starting address of the list must be in DI. MINMAX returns the maximum value in AX and the minimum value in BX.

This procedure has three parts. The first part calculates the number of comparisons to make (element count − 1) and sets up the first data element as both the maximum and minimum norm. The second and third parts loop through the list searching for a new minimum and a new maximum, respectively. New minimums are loaded into BX; new maximums are loaded into AX.

This particular procedure processes lists of *unsigned* word values, but you easily modify it to search for the maximum and minimum in a list of *signed* words. In Example 5–3, simply replace JAE NOMIN with JGE NOMIN and replace JBE NOMAX with JLE NOMAX. For the reason behind this, see Table 3–11 in Section 3.7.

Example 5–3. Maximum and Minimum Values in an Unordered List

```
; This procedure finds the maximum and minimum
; word values in an unordered list in the extra
; segment, and returns those values in AX and BX,
; respectively. The starting address of the list
; is in DI. The length of the list, in words, is
; in the list's first location. DI is returned
; unaltered.
MINMAX    PROC
          PUSH DI              ;Save starting
                               ; address
          MOV   CX,ES:[DI]     ;Fetch word count
          DEC   CX             ;Get ready for count-
                               ; 1 comparisons
          PUSH CX              ;Save this count
                               ; value
          MOV   BX,ES:[DI+2]   ;To start, make first
                               ; element minimum
          MOV   AX,BX          ; and maximum
;
; These instructions find the minimum value in
;    the list.
;
          ADD   DI,4           ;Point to second
                               ; element in the
                               ; list
          PUSH DI              ; and save this
                               ; pointer
CHKMIN:   CMP   ES:[DI],BX     ;Compare next element
                               ; to minimum
          JAE   NOMIN          ;New minimum found?
          MOV   BX,ES:[DI]     ; Yes. Put it in BX
```

```
NOMIN:    ADD    DI,2             ;Point to next
                                  ; element
          LOOP CHKMIN             ;Check entire list
; These instructions find the maximum value in
;   the list.
;
          POP    DI               ;Point to second
                                  ; element in the
                                  ; list
          POP    CX               Reload comparison
                                  ; counter
CHKMAX:   CMP    ES:[DI],AX       ;Compare next element
                                  ; to maximum
          JBE    NOMAX            ;New maximum found?
          MOV    AX,ES:[DI]       ; Yes. Put it in AX
NOMAX:    ADD    DI,2             ;Point to next
                                  ; element
          LOOP CHKMAX             ;Check entire list
          RET
MINMAX    ENDP
```

5.2 Sorting Unordered Data

If you are plotting information versus time or processing text, you can accept the information in unordered form. In many applications, however, it is better to have the information arranged in increasing or decreasing order, because it is easier to analyze that way.

How can you rearrange a list of unordered data? There is a considerable amount of literature on this subject, but we'll concentrate on one common sorting technique called the *bubble sort*. If you want to investigate other sorting techniques, D. E. Knuth's classic *The Art of Computer Programming. Volume 3: Sorting and Searching* (Addison-Wesley) is an excellent starting point.

Bubble Sort

The bubble sort technique is so named because it makes list elements "rise" upward in memory (to higher-numbered addresses) like soap bubbles rise in the air. A bubble sort accesses elements in a list sequentially, starting with the first element, and compares each element to the next one in the list.

If the bubble sort program finds an element that is greater than its higher-addressed neighbor, it exchanges these elements. It then compares the next two elements, exchanges them if required, and so on.

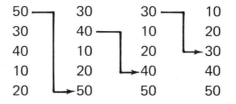

**Figure 5–2. A bubble sort "bubbles"
the largest numbers to the end.**

By the time the 8086 gets to the last element, the highest-valued element will have "bubbled-up" to that final list position.

In sorting with this algorithm, the processor usually makes several passes through the list, as you can see from the simple example in Figure 5–2. Here, the first pass "bubbles" 50 to the end of the list and the next two passes bubble 40 and 30 to the next highest positions. Therefore, this particular list gets sorted in three passes.

Seeing pass-by-pass "snapshots" of the list, as in Figure 5–2, makes it easy for *you* to know when a list is entirely sorted, but how can a *computer* know when a list is sorted? Unless you give it a specific pass count, or tell it when to stop in some other way, the computer will go merrily along, executing pass after pass, ad infinitum. Since the number of sorting passes depends on the initial arrangement of the list, we have no way of providing an exact pass count in a program. As an alternative, we will set up a special indicator, called an *exchange flag*, that the computer can use to find out when to stop sorting.

The exchange flag is set to 1 before each sorting pass. Any sorting pass that includes an element exchange operation changes the exchange flag to 0. Therefore, after each pass, the value of the exchange flags tells the computer whether to continue sorting. A value of 0 tells it to make another pass through the list. A value of 1 indicates the list is sorted, and tells it to stop sorting. Figure 5–3 shows a flowchart of the bubble sort algorithm.

As you can see, even if a list is already in order at the outset, it takes the processor one pass to deduce this fact. If one pass is the minimum, what *maximum* number of passes may you anticipate? Since the five-number list in Figure 5–2 was already partially sorted, we made only three sorting passes to put it in ascending order. One more pass is needed to detect that this list is indeed sorted, making four passes altogether.

If that list had been arranged initially in descending order (the worst case), the processor would have made five passes through the list— four passes to sort the data and one more pass to determine no further sorting was needed. From this observation, we can state that *an N-element list takes from one to N passes to sort, with (N + 1)/2 passes being the average.*

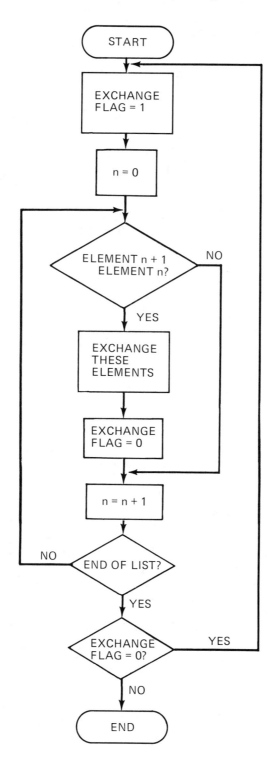

Figure 5–3. The bubble sort algorithm.

A Bubble Sort Program

With the preceding background in bubble sort theory and a flowchart showing what needs to be done, we are prepared to write a program that sorts a list in memory. Example 5–4 shows a procedure (B_SORT) that sorts a list of word values, although you can easily modify it to sort a list of bytes.

As usual, the list lies in the extra segment, and is addressed by DI. B_SORT uses BX to hold the exchange flag (which always holds a value of either 1 or 0) and AX to hold the element value that is being compared to the next element in the list.

Example 5–4. A Bubble Sort Procedure

```
; This procedure arranges the 16-bit elements of
; a list in ascending order in memory, using
; bubble sort. The list is in the extra segment,
; and its starting address is in DI. The length
; of the list, in words, is in the list's first
; location. DI is returned unaltered. Set up
; these variables in the data segment.
;
SAVE_CNT     DW  ?
START_ADDR   DW  ?
;
B_SORT  PROC
        PUSH    AX                  ;Save scratch
        PUSH    BX                  ; registers on stack
        MOV     START_ADDR,DI       ;Save starting
                                    ; address in memory
        MOV     CX,ES:[DI]          ;Fetch element count
        DEC     CX                  ;Get ready for
                                    ; count-1
                                    ; comparisons
        MOV     SAVE_CNT,CX         ;Save this value in
                                    ; memory
INIT:   MOV     BX,1                ;Exchange flag
                                    ; (BX) = 1
        MOV     CX,SAVE_CNT         ;Load count into CX
        MOV     DI,START_ADDR       ; and start address
                                    ; into DI
NEXT:   ADD     DI,2                ;Address a data
                                    ; element
        MOV     AX,ES:[DI]          ; and load it into
                                    ; AX
        CMP     ES:[DI+2],AX        ;Is next element <
                                    ; this element?
        JAE     CONT                ; No. Check next
                                    ; pair
```

```
          XCHG    ES:[DI+2],AX      ; Yes. Exchange
                                    ; these elements
          MOV     ES:[DI],AX
          SUB     BX,BX             ;  and make
                                    ;     exchange flag 0
CONT:     LOOP    NEXT              ;Process entire list
          CMP     BX,0              ;Were any exchanges
                                    ; made?
          JE      INIT              ; If so, make
                                    ; another pass
          MOV     DI,START_ADDR     ; If not, restore
                                    ; registers
          POP     BX
          POP     AX
          RET                       ; and exit.
B_SORT    ENDP
```

The B_SORT procedure also uses two word variables in the data segment: *SAVE_CNT* holds the comparison count (element count − 1) and *START_ADDR* holds the starting address of the list. B_SORT uses these variables to reinitialize CX and DI at the beginning of each new sort operation.

Although it has a lot of instructions, the B_SORT procedure is quite simple. After calculating the values for SAVE_CNT and START_ADDR, the procedure initializes the exchange flag (BX = 1), the comparison counter (CX), and the element pointer (DI). At the label NEXT, the 8086 loads an element into AX, then compares it with the next element in memory.

If the second element is less than the first, the 8086 loads the second element into AX and stores the two elements back into memory, in reverse order. Because an exchange took place, the processor clears BX to zero. The LOOP instruction at CONT transfers control back to NEXT until the entire list has been processed.

When all elements have been compared, and exchanged as needed, a CMP instruction checks whether the exchange flag (BX) is zero. If it is, at least one exchange took place during the preceding sorting pass, so the 8086 jumps back to INIT to begin a new pass. Otherwise, if BX is still 1 after a sorting pass, the list is finally sorted, so the 8086 restores DI from START_ADDR and BX and AX from the stack, then returns.

Streamlining the Bubble Sort Program

The bubble sort procedure in Example 5–4 has one subtle, but noteworthy, deficiency: it sorts some elements needlessly. To be specific, during each sorting pass B_SORT compares every pair of elements in the list. However, each pass makes an element "bubble" higher in the list. The first pass bubbles the highest-valued element to the end of the list, the second pass bubbles the next highest-valued element to the next-to-last proper position, and so on. Therefore, the elements at the end of the list are in their final (sorted) positions, so you may exclude them from subsequent sorting passes!

To exclude these sorted elements, *each pass through the list should involve one less comparison than the preceding pass.* We can make this happen by modifying our procedure so that the value in SAVE_CNT gets decremented before each new pass. Fortunately, this change is very easy to make.

To do this, you need to change the sixth, seventh, and eighth instructions in the procedure to bring the decrement-count operation under the label INIT. You also need to add one more instruction after the decrement, to make the processor exit if SAVE_CNT is 0. Here is a summary of the changes:

Old	Revised
DEX CX	MOV SAVE_CNT,CX
MOV SAVE_CNT,CX	INIT: MOV BX,1
INIT: MOV BX,1	DEC SAVE_CNT
	JZ SORTED

Here, SORTED refers to the MOV instruction that restores the contents of DI from START_ADDR. The bubble sort procedure that has these changes (BUBBLE) is shown in Example 5–5.

For any given list, BUBBLE makes the same number of sorting passes as the B_SORT procedure in Example 5–4. But BUBBLE makes about half as many *comparisons* as B_SORT, so BUBBLE executes much faster than B_SORT.

For instance, in sorting 100 elements arranged in decreasing order, B_SORT makes 100 passes, with 99 comparisons in each pass—a total of 9,900 comparisons. By contrast, BUBBLE makes 100 passes, with 99 comparisons in the first pass and one comparison in the last pass, for an average of 50 comparisons—a total of 5,500 comparisons.

To compare BUBBLE and B_SORT, I sorted two lists of 16-bit elements using both procedures on an IBM Personal Computer, which has a 4.77-MHz 8088 processor. Both lists were initially arranged in decreasing order. The first list, which had 500 elements, was sorted in 7.5 seconds by B_SORT and in 4.5 seconds by BUBBLE. The second list, which had 1,000 elements, was sorted in 28.0 seconds by B_SORT and in 16.5 seconds by BUBBLE. Based on these tests, we can assume that *BUBBLE sorts a list about 40 percent faster than B_SORT.*

Example 5–5. A Better Bubble Sort Procedure

```
; This procedure arranges the 16-bit elements of
; a list in ascending order in memory, using
```

```
; bubble sort. The list is in the extra segment,
; and its starting address is in DI. The length
; of the list, in words, is in the list's first
; location. DI is returned unaltered. Set up
; these variables in the data segment.
;
SAVE_CNT      DW ?
START_ADDR    DW ?
;
BUBBLE  PROC
        PUSH  AX                  ;Save scratch
                                  ; registers on stack
        PUSH  BX
        MOV   START_ADDR,DI       ;Save starting
                                  ; address in memory
        MOV   CX,ES:[DI]          ;Fetch element count
        MOV   SAVE_CNT,CX         ;Save this value in
                                  ; memory
INIT:   MOV   BX,1                ;Exchange flag
                                  ; (BX) = 1
        DEC   SAVE_CNT            ;Get ready for
                                  ; count-1
                                  ; comparisons
        JZ    SORTED              ;Exit if SAVE_CNT is
                                  ; 0
        MOV   CX,SAVE_CNT         ;Load the compare
                                  ; count into CX
        MOV   DI,START_ADDR       ; and the start
                                  ; address into DI
NEXT:   ADD   DI,2                ;Address a data
                                  ; element
        MOV   AX,ES:[DI]          ; and load it into
                                  ; AX
        CMP   ES:[DI+2],AX        ;Is next element <
                                  ; this element?
        JAE   CONT                ; No. Check next
                                  ; pair
        XCHG  ES:[DI+2],AX        ; Yes. Exchange
                                  ; these elements
        MOV   ES:[DI],AX
        SUB   BX,BX               ; and make exchange
                                  ; flag 0
CONT:   LOOP  NEXT                ;Process entire list
        CMP   BX,0                ;Were any exchanges
                                  ; made?
        JE    INIT                ; If so, make
                                  ; another pass
SORTED: MOV   DI,START_ADDR       ; If not, restore
                                  ; registers
        POP   BX
```

```
          POP   AX
          RET                    ;  and exit.
BUBBLE    ENDP
```

Note that the sorting time rises dramatically as you take on longer lists. The bubble sort procedures presented here can sort lists up to 32K words long, but you'd better be prepared to wait if your list is that extensive. In fact, on the IBM PC, a "worst-case" list of even 2,000 words takes BUBBLE about 66 seconds to sort.

5.3 Ordered Lists

Now that you know how to sort a list, let us discuss how to search for a known value, and then see how to add and delete elements.

Searching An Ordered List

In Section 5.1 we learned that to locate a given value in an unordered list, you must search the list sequentially, element by element. This takes an average of N/2 comparisons for an N-element list. If a list is *ordered*, however, you can use any of several search techniques to find a value. For all but the shortest lists, most of these techniques are faster and more efficient than searching sequentially.

The Binary Search

One of the most common techniques for searching ordered lists is the *binary search*. Its name reflects the fact that it divides the list into a series of progressively shorter halves ("bi" is Latin for "two"), and eventually closes in on one element location in the list. A binary search starts in the middle of the list and determines whether the search value lies above or below that point. It then takes *that* half of the list and divides *it* into halves, and so on.

The flowchart in Figure 5–4 shows how you make a binary search on an ordered list. The result of the search is an address. If the search value is in the list, the address is that of the matching element. If the value is not in the list, the address is that of the last location to be compared. Of course, the program that performs this search must also return some kind of indicator that tells you whether the address reflects a successful search or an unsuccessful search.

Example 5–6 shows a procedure (B_SEARCH) you can use to search an ordered list of unsigned words. The fact that this procedure operates on words instead of bytes requires us to make a few changes to our basic algorithm. For one thing, because words lie 2 bytes apart in mem-

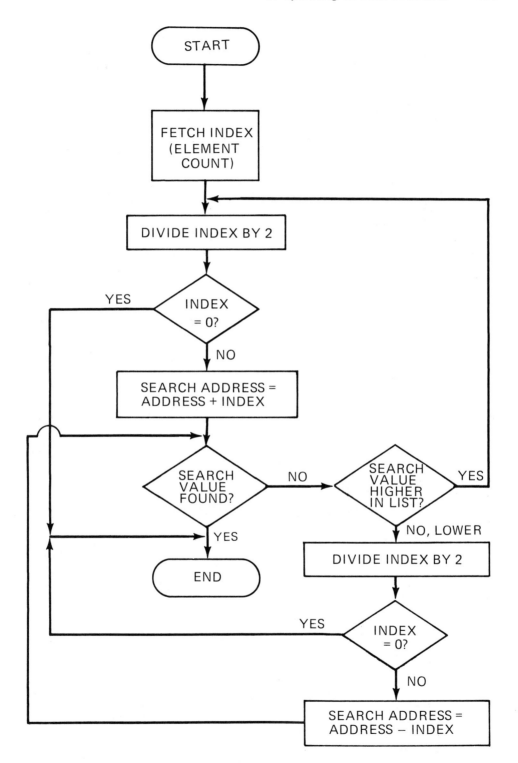

Figure 5–4. Binary search algorithm.

ory, we must include instructions that ensure the index is always a multiple of two, that is, an *even* value. For the same reason, we terminate a search, and declare it unsuccessful, when the index has decreased to 2 (instead of 0).

Example 5–6. A 16-Bit Binary Search Procedure

```
; This procedure searches an ordered list in the
; extra segment for the word value contained in
; AX.
; The starting address of the list is in DI. The
; length of the list, in words, is in the list's
; first location. .
; The results are returned in SI and the Carry
; Flag (CF), as follows:
;       1. If the value is in the list, CF is 0
;          and SI holds the address of the
;          matching element.
;       2. If the value is not in the list, CF is
;          1 and SI holds the address of the last
;          element to be compared.
; In either case, AX and DI are unaffected.
;
; Set up this variable in memory.
;
START_ADDR   DW   ?
;
B_SEARCH     PROC
;
; First find out if AX lies beyond the
; boundaries of the list.
;
             CMP   AX,ES:[DI+2]    ;Search value <
                                   ; or = first
                                   ; element?
             JA    CHK_LAST        ; No. Check last
                                   ; element
             LEA   SI,ES:[DI+2]    ; Yes. Fetch
                                   ; address of
                                   ;  first element.
             JE    EXIT_1ST        ;If value = first
                                   ; element, exit
             STC                   ;If value < first
                                   ; element, set CF
EXIT_1ST:    RET
CHK_LAST:    MOV   SI,ES:[DI]      ;Point to last
                                   ; element
             SHL   SI,1
             ADD   SI,DI
             CMP   AX,ES:[SI]      ;Search value >
                                   ; or = last
                                   ; element?
```

```
              JB    SEARCH              ; No. Search list
              JE    EXIT_LAST           ; Yes. Exit if
                                        ; value = element
              STC                       ;If value > last
                                        ; element, set CF
EXIT_LAST:    RET
;
;  Search for the value within the list.
;
SEARCH:       MOV   START_ADDR,DI       ;Save starting
                                        ; address in
                                        ; memory
              MOV   SI,ES:[DI]          ;Fetch index
EVEN_INDX;    TEST  SI,1                ;Force index to
                                        ; an even value
              JZ    ADD_IDX
              INC   SI
ADD_IDX:      ADD   DI,SI               ;Calculate next
                                        ; search address
COMPARE:      CMP   AX,ES:[DI]          ;Search value
                                        ; found?
              JE    ALL_DONE            ; If so, exit
              JA    HIGHER              ; Otherwise, find
                                        ; correct half
;
;  Search lower in the list.
;
              CMP   SI,2                ;Index = 2?
              JNE   IDX_OK
NO_MATCH:     STC                       ; If so, set CF
              JE    ALL_DONE            ; and exit
IDX_OK:       SHR   SI,1                ; If not, divide
                                        ; index by 2
              TEST  SI,1                ;Force index to
                                        ; an even value
              JZ    SUB_IDX
              INC   SI
SUB_IDX       SUB   DI,SI               ;Calculate next
                                        ; address
              JMP   SHORT COMPARE       ;Check this
                                        ; element
;
;  Search higher in the list.
;
HIGHER:       CMP   SI,2                ;Index = 2?
              JE    NO_MATCH            ; If so, set CF
                                        ; and exit
              SHR   SI,1                ; If not, divide
                                        ; index by 2
              JMP   SHORT EVEN_IDX      ; and check next
                                        ; element
```

```
;
;  These are the exit instructions.
;
ALL_DONE:    MOV   SI,DI             ;Move compare
                                     ; address into SI
             MOV   DI,START_ADDR     ;Restore starting
                                     ; address
             RET                     ; and exit
B_SEARCH:    ENDP
```

In this procedure, the search value is in AX and the starting address of the list is in DI. B_SEARCH returns the result address in SI, and CF tells whether the value was found (CF = 0) or not found (CF = 1).

The B_SEARCH procedure begins with a step that is not included in the basic binary search algorithm (Figure 5–5): it compares the search value with the first and last elements in the list. If the search value is less than the first element or greater than the last element, or if it matches one of those elements, the procedure terminates without further ado. If these initial checks fail, however, the 8086 proceeds to the search operation, starting at SEARCH.

Once DI is saved in memory, the 8086 copies the index (word count) from the first location of the list into SI, and forces it to an even value, if appropriate. This index is added to DI to form the address of the middle element in the list, the starting point for the binary search. The 8086 then compares the search value to this middle element, and jumps to ALL_DONE if the values match. In the absence of a match, the 8086 determines whether to continue its search in the upper half of the list (the instructions that start at HIGHER) or the lower half of the list.

These paths are similar in that both do the following:

1. Check whether the index is equal to 2. If it is, the 8086 sets CF to 1 (to indicate a nonmatch), then transfers to ALL_DONE to exit.
2. Divide the index by 2 by shifting it right one position.
3. Force the shifted index to an even value.

To search lower in the list, however, the 8086 subtracts the index (SI) from the current address (DI); to search higher in the list, it adds the index to the current address.

This process repeats until the index has diminished to 2 or the search value is found. Either way, the procedure ends at ALL_DONE, where DI is moved to SI and the original contents of DI are retrieved from memory.

How much more efficient is a binary search than a straight sequential, element-by-element scan—the kind we used in Examples 5–1 and 5–2? In his article "An Introduction to Algorithm Design" (*Computer*, February 1979, pp. 66–78), Jon L. Bentley stated that while a sequential search of an N-element list requires an average of N/2 comparisons, a binary search requires an average of $\log_2 N$ comparisons. Therefore, sequentially scanning a 100-element list will average 50 comparisons, but a binary search will do the same job with about seven comparisons!

Of course, you normally search a list for a value in order to *do* something to the matching element. Typically, you either want to add the value to the list or delete it from the list. Let's see how to perform those operations.

Adding an Element to an Ordered List

You add an element to an ordered list with four basic steps:

1. Find out where the value should be added.
2. Clear a location for the entry by moving all higher-valued elements down one position.
3. Insert the entry at the newly-vacated element position.
4. Add to the list's element count, to reflect the insertion.

The B_SEARCH procedure we just developed gives us a good clue as to where the entry should be added, in that it returns the address of the element where the search stopped. To complete Step 1, we need to determine whether the entry must be inserted just *before* or just *after* that final search element. You make that determination by comparing the entry value to the final search element.

Example 5–7 shows a procedure (ADD_TO_OL) that performs the four steps we just listed. This procedure begins by calling B_SEARCH, to find out whether the entry value is already in the list. As you know, B_SEARCH returns an address in SI and a found/not-found indicator in the Carry Flag (CF).

Example 5–7. Adding an Element to an Ordered List

```
; This procedure adds the value in AX to an
; ordered list in the extra segment, if the
; value is not already in the list.
; The starting address of the list is in DI. The
; length of the list, in words, is in the list's
; first location.
; Neither AX nor DI is affected.
; The B_SEARCH procedure (Example 5-6) is used
; to conduct the search.
;
ADD_TO_OL    PROC
             PUSH  SI              ;Save SI and BX
             PUSH  BX
             CALL  B_SEARCH        ;Is the value
                                   ; in the list?
```

```
                  JNC    GOODBYE            ; If so, exit
                  MOV    BX,SI              ; If not, copy
                                            ; compare
                                            ; address to BX
                  MOV    CX,ES:[DI]         ;Find address
                                            ; of last
                                            ; element

                  SHL    CX,1
                  ADD    CX,DI              ;   and put it
                                            ;    in CX
                  PUSH   CX                 ;Save end
                                            ; address on
                                            ; the stack
                  SUB    CX,SI              ;Calculate no.
                                            ; of words to
                                            ; be moved

                  SHR    CX,1
                  CMP    AX,ES:[SI]         ;Should compare
                                            ; element be
                                            ; moved, too?

                  JA     EXCLUDE
                  INC    CX                 ; Yes. Increase
                                            ; move count by
                                            ; 1

                  JNZ    CHECK_CNT
EXCLUDE:          ADD    BX,2               ; No. Adjust
                                            ; insert
                                            ; pointer

CHECK_CNT:        CMP    CX,0               ;Move count =
                                            ; 0?

                  JNE    MOVE_ELS
                  POP    SI                 ; If so, store
                                            ; value at end
                                            ; of list,

                  MOV    ES:[SI+2],AX
                  JMP    SHORT INC_CNT      ; then increase
                                            ; element count
MOVE_ELS:         POP    SI                 ;Start move at
                                            ; end of list
                  PUSH   BX                 ;Save insert
                                            ; address on
                                            ; stack
MOVE_ONE:         MOV    BX,ES:[SI]         ;Move one
                                            ; element down
                                            ; in list

                  MOV    ES:[SI+2],BX
                  SUB    SI,2               ;Point to next
                                            ; element
                  LOOP   MOVE_ONE           ;Repeat until
                                            ; all are moved
```

```
              POP    BX                    ;Retrieve
                                           ;  insert
                                           ;  address
              MOV    ES:[BX],AX            ;Insert AX in
                                           ;  the list
INC_CNT:      INC    WORD PTR ES:[DI]      ;Add 1 to
                                           ;  element
                                           ;  count
GOODBYE:      POP    BX                    ;Restore
                                           ;  registers
              POP    SI
              RET                          ;  and exit
ADD_TO_OL     ENDP
```

Upon return from B_SEARCH, the ADD_TO_OL procedure interrogates CF, and exits if CF is 0 (since that means the entry is already in the list). If CF is 1, however, the procedure saves the last-searched address in BX and calculates the address of the last element (in CX). Subtracting the contents of SI from this address gives the number of bytes that must be moved higher in memory to make room for the insertion. Right-shifting this result (that is, dividing it by 2) tells you how many *words* to move. If the entry value is less than the last-compared element, that element must also be moved, so the move count (CX) is increased by 1.

At CHECK_CNT, the 8086 checks whether the move count is zero. If it is, the entry is simply tacked on to the end of the list. Otherwise, this value must be inserted in the list, which requires moving all subsequent elements down one word position.

The instructions starting at MOVE_ELS move elements down, one by one, starting with the last word in the list. When all required elements have been moved, the 8086 inserts the entry (AX) in the newly-vacated slot, then increases the element count by 1.

Deleting an Element from an Ordered List

It is much easier to delete an element from an ordered list than it is to add one, because all we must do is find the proper element, move all subsequent elements up one location, and decrement the element count.

Example 5–8 shows a typical delete procedure (DEL_OL), which uses B_SEARCH (see Example 5–6) to locate the intended deletion "victim." As usual, the starting address of the list is in DI and the value to be deleted is in AX.

If B_SEARCH locates the entry value in the list, DEL_OL uses its address, and the address of the end of the list, to find out how many words must be moved up in memory. The four-instruction loop at MOVEM performs the move operation. When the 8086 has moved all words, it decreases the list's element count to reflect the deletion.

Example 5–8. Deleting an Element from an Ordered List

```
; This procedure deletes the value in AX from an
; ordered list in the extra segment, if the
; value is in the list.
; The starting address of the list is in DI. The
; length of the list, in words, is in the list's
; first location.
; Neither AX nor DI is affected.
; The B_SEARCH procedure (Example 5-6) is used
; to conduct the search.
;
DEL_OL    PROC
          PUSH    SI              ;Save SI and BX
          PUSH    BX
          CALL    B_SEARCH        ;Is the value in
                                  ; the list?
          JC      ADIOS           ; If not, exit
          MOV     CX,ES:[DI]      ; If so, find
                                  ; address of last
                                  ; element
          SHL     CX,1
          ADD     CX,DI           ; and put it in
                                  ; CX
          CMP     CX,SI           ;Is the last
                                  ; element to be
                                  ; deleted?
          JE      CNT_M1          ; Yes. Decrement
                                  ; element count
          SUB     CX,SI           ; No. Calculate
                                  ; move count
          SHR     EX,1
MOVEM:    MOV     BX,ES:[SI+2]    ;Move one element
                                  ; up in list
          MOV     ES:[SI],BX
          ADD     SI,2            ;Point to next
                                  ; element
          LOOP    MOVEM           ;Repeat until all
                                  ; are moved
CNT_M1:   DEC     WORD PTR ES:[DI] ;Decrease element
                                  ; count by 1
ADIOS:    POP     BX              ;Restore
                                  ; registers
          POP     SI
          RET                     ; and exit
DEL_OL    ENDP
```

5.4 Look-Up Tables

Many applications use tables to hold values that are needed during processing. In some applications, these tables hold numbers—such as sines of angles—that take too much time to derive mathematically. In other applications, tables hold parameters that have some defined relationship to a program input, but which cannot be calculated. For instance, you can't give the computer someone's name and expect it to calculate his or her telephone number.

Applications like these call for a *look-up table*. As the name implies, a look-up table obtains an item of information (an *argument*) based on a known value (a *function*).

Look-up tables can replace complicated or time-consuming conversion operations, such as extracting the square root or cube root of a number, or deriving a trigonometric function (sine, cosine, and so on) of an angle. Look-up tables are especially efficient when a function covers only a small range of arguments. By using a look-up table, the microcomputer doesn't need to perform complex calculations each time a function is required.

Look-up tables reduce the execution time in all but the simplest relationships. (For instance, you wouldn't use a look-up table to store arguments that are always twice the value of a function.) But since look-up tables usually take up large amounts of memory storage space, they are most efficient in applications where you are willing to sacrifice memory space for execution speed.

Because look-up applications are so common, the 8086 has a special instruction, *Translate (XLAT)*, for this purpose. XLAT looks up a value in a byte table, using the contents of BX as a base address and the contents of AL as an index into the table, and returns the addressed byte value in AL. This section includes examples of look-up operations on both byte tables and word tables.

Look-Up Tables Can Replace Equations

You can save processing time and program development time by providing the results of complex equations in a look-up table. As typical examples, we will examine how look-up tables can provide the sine or cosine of an angle.

Sine of an Angle

As you may recall from high school trigonometry, the sine of all angles between 0° and 360° can be graphed, as shown in Figure 5–5A. Math-

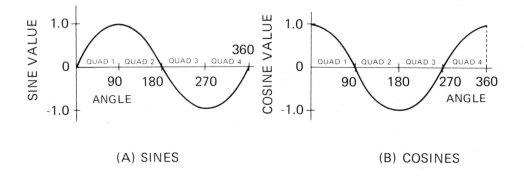

Figure 5–5. The sines and cosines of angles between 0 and 360 degrees.

ematically, you can approximate this curve with the formula

$$sine(x) = X - \frac{X^3}{3!} + \frac{X^5}{5!} - \frac{X^7}{7!} + \frac{X^9}{9!} \ldots$$

It is possible to write a program to make this calculation, but such a program would probably require a few milliseconds to execute. If your application requires very precise sines, you may be forced to write such a program, but most applications are better served by an angle-to-sine look-up table.

If an application needs the sine of any angle between 0° and 360°, where the angle is an integer in degrees, how many sine values must the table contain? 360 sine values? No, we can get by with a table of only *91 sine values*—one value for each angle between 0° and 90°.

To understand how this can be so, look at Figure 5–5A again. If we call the leftmost quarter of the graph (angles from 0° to 90°) Quadrant 1, we see that:

1. Sines in Quadrant 2 (91° to 180°) are the "mirror image" of those in Quadrant 1.
2. Sines in Quadrant 3 (181° to 270°) are the "negative inverse" of those in Quadrant 1.
3. Sines in Quadrant 4 (271° to 360°) are the "negative inverse, mirror image" of those in Quadrant 1.

That is, the sines in Quadrants 2, 3, and 4 bear some simple relationship to those in Quadrant 1.

Therefore, if you store the values in Quadrant 1 in a look-up table, your program can find the sine of an angle in any quadrant by making these conversions:

If the angle X is between	**Take**
0° and 90°	Sine(X)
91° and 180°	Sine(180 − X)

| 181° and 270° | $-\text{Sine}(X - 180)$ |
| 271° and 360° | $-\text{Sine}(360 - X)$ |

These relationships let us construct a flowchart for an angle-to-sine conversion program. This flowchart, shown in Figure 5–6, derives the sine as a sign-and-magnitude value. That is, the high-order bit of the result gives the sign of the sine (0 = positive, 1 = negative) and the remaining low-order bits give the sine's magnitude (its absolute value).

Example 5–9 gives an angle-to-sine look-up procedure called *FIND_ SINE*. This procedure accepts angles from 0° to 360° in AX and returns a 16-bit sign-and-magnitude sine value in BX. In the look-up table (SINES), the sines are stored as integers. You must divide them by 10,000 if you want to use them as operands.

At the beginning of this procedure, the 8086 checks whether the angle is less than 181°. If it is, the processor jumps to SIN_POS; otherwise, it sets the most-significant bit of a sign register (CX) to 1—because sines above 180° are negative—and subtracts 180 from the angle.

Example 5–9. Look-Up the Sine of an Angle

```
; This procedure returns the sine of the angle
; (0 to 360 degrees) contained in AX.
; The sine, a sign-and-magnitude value, is
; returned in BX. The contents of AX are
; unaffected.
;
; Store this sine look-up table in the data
; segment.
;

SINES   DW   0,175,349,523,698,872              ;0-5
        DW   1045,1219,1392,1564,1736           ;6-10
        DW   1908,2079,2250,2419,2588           ;11-15
        DW   2756,2924,3090,3256,3420           ;16-20
        DW   3584,3746,3907,4067,4226           ;21-25
        DW   4384,4540,4695,4848,5000           ;26-30
        DW   5150,5299,5446,5592,5736           ;31-35
        DW   5878,6018,6157,6293,6428           ;36-40
        DW   6561,6691,6820,6947,7071           ;41-45
        DW   7193,7313,7431,7547,7660           ;46-50
        DW   7771,7880,7986,8090,8191           ;51-55
        DW   8290,8387,8480,8572,8660           ;56-60
        DW   8746,8829,8910,8988,9063           ;61-65
        DW   9135,9205,9272,9336,9397           ;66-70
        DW   9455,9511,9563,9613,9659           ;71-75
        DW   9703,9744,9781,9816,9848           ;76-80
        DW   9877,9903,9926,9945,9962           ;81-85
        DW   9976,9986,9994,9998,10000          ;86-90
```

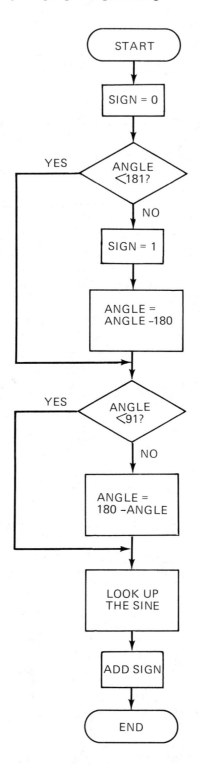

Figure 5–6. Flowchart for
angle-to-sine conversion
program.

```
;
; This is the look-up procedure.
;
FIND_SINE    PROC
             PUSH    AX                      ;Save AX
             PUSH    CX                      ; and CX
             SUB     CX,CX                   ;Initialize sign
                                             ; to 0
             CMP     AX,181                  ;Angle < 181
                                             ; degrees?
             JB      SIN_POS                 ; Yes. Continue
                                             ; with sign = 0
             MOV     CX,8000H                ; No. Set sign =
                                             ; 1
             SUB     AX,180                  ; and subtract
                                             ; 180 from angle
SIN_POS:     CMP     AX,91                   ;Angle < 91
                                             ; degrees?
             JB      GET_SIN                 ; Yes. Look up
                                             ; sine
             NEG     AX                      ; No. Subtract
                                             ; angle from 180
             ADD     AX,180
GET_SIN:     MOV     BX,AX                   ;Make angle a
                                             ; word index
             SHL     BX,1
             MOV     BX,SINES[BX]            ; and look up the
                                             ; sine value
             OR      BX,CX                   ;Combine sine
                                             ; with sign bit
             POP     CX
             POP     AX
             RET
FIND_SINE    ENDP
```

With the correct sign now in Bit 15 of CX, the CMP instruction at SIN_POS compares the input angle to 91°. If the angle is greater than or equal to 91°, its value must be subtracted from 180. You would expect to perform this subtraction with the instruction SUB 180,AX, but the 8086 does not offer this form.

That being the case, we make the subtraction by negating AX, then adding 180 to the result. The four instructions at GET_SIN load the angle into BX, double it to form a word index, look up the sine in SINES, and OR it with the sign in CX.

How long FIND_SINE takes to return a sine value depends on which quadrant the angle is in. The execution times (excluding the time required to execute the CALL and RET instructions) are as follows:

• For angles between 0° and 90°, FIND_SINE executes in 125 cycles.
• For angles between 91° and 180°, FIND_SINE executes in 120 cycles.

• For angles between 181° and 270°, FIND_SINE executes in 121 cycles.
• For angles between 271° and 360°, FIND_SINE executes in 116 cycles.

Cosine of an Angle

As Figure 5–5B shows, the cosine curve is nothing more than the sine curve displaced one quadrant to the left. Therefore, the cosine of any given angle is equal to the sine of an angle that is 90° greater. That is,

```
cosine(X) = sine(X+90)
```

Knowing this, we can use the SINES table in Example 5–9 to look up the cosine of an angle as well as its sine. Example 5–10 shows a procedure that does this. As with FIND_SINE, you must divide the result of FIND_COS by 10,000.

Incidentally, note that the sine and cosine curves are symmetric about the vertical axis, so sines and cosines of negative angles have the same magnitudes as their positive counterparts. For example, the sine and cosine of −25° have the same magnitudes as those of +25°. This means you can also use FIND_SINE and FIND_COS for angles between −1° and −360° by supplying the angle's *absolute value* in AX.

Example 5–10. Look Up the Cosine of an Angle

```
; This procedure returns the cosine of the angle
; (0 to 360 degrees) contained in AX.
; The cosine, a sign-and-magnitude value, is
; returned in BX.
; The contents of AX are unaffected.
; This procedure calls FIND_SINE (Example 5-9).
;
FIND_COS   PROC
           PUSH   AX            ;Save AX
           ADD    AX,90         ;Add 90 for use by
                                ; FIND_SINE
           CMP    AX,360        ;Is the result
                                ; greater than 360?
           JNA    GET_COS
           SUB    AX,360        ; If so, subtract 360
GET_COS:   CALL   FIND_SINE     ;Look-up the cosine
           POP    AX
           RET
FIND_COS   ENDP
```

Look-Up Tables Can Perform Code Conversions

Look-up tables can also hold coded data such as display codes, printer codes, and messages. Example 5–11 shows a procedure that performs multiple look-ups; it converts a hexadecimal digit in AL to its ASCII, BCD, and EBCDIC equivalents. The converted values are returned in CH, CL, and AH, respectively.

Example 5-11. Convert Hex to ASCII, BCD, and EBCDIC

```
; This procedure converts a hexadecimal digit in
; AL to its ASCII, BCD, and EBCDIC equivalents.
; The converted values are returned in CH, CL,
; and AH, respectively.
; The contents of AL are unaffected.
;
; These look-up tables must be stored in the
; data segment.
;
ASCII   DB  '0123456789ABCDEF'
BCD     DB  0,1,2,3,4,5,6,7,8,9,10H,
            11H,12H,13H,14H,15H
EBCDIC  DB  0F0H,0F1H,0F2H,0F3H,0F4H,0F5H,
            0F6H,0F7H
        DB  0F8H,0F9H,0C1H,0C2H,0C3H,0C4H,
            0C5H,0C6H

;
;  Here is the conversion procedure.
;
CONV_HEX   PROC
           PUSH  BX              ;Save BX and DX
           PUSH  DX
           MOV   DL,AL           ;Save the input value
                                 ; in DL
           LEA   BX,ASCII        ;Look-up the ASCII
                                 ; value
           XLAT  ASCII
           MOV   CH,AL           ; and load it into CH
           MOV   AL,DL
           LEA   BX,BCD          ;Look-up the BCD value
           XLAT  BCD
           MOV   CL,AL           ; and load it into CL
           MOV   AL,DL
           LEA   BX,EBCDIC       ;Look-up the EBCDIC
                                 ; value
           XLAT  EBCDIC
           MOV   AH,AL           ; and load it into AH
           MOV   AL,DL           ;Restore registers
           POP   DX
           POP   BX
           RET
CONV_HEX   ENDP
```

When you transmit data between the computer and a printer, display, or some other peripheral in the system, it takes a form called *ASCII* (for American Standard Code for Information Interchange). *EBCDIC* (Extended Binary-Coded Decimal Interchange Code) is a transmission protocol for data processing and communications systems.

Jump Tables

Some look-up tables contain *addresses* rather than data values. For instance, an error routine may use a look-up table to find the starting address of one particular message in a set of possible messages. Similarly, an interrupt service routine may use a look-up table to call one of several interrupt handler programs, depending on which type of service a particular device requested. Another routine may use a look-up table to call one of several control programs, based on which control key an operator pressed. In all of these applications (and there are many more), the look-up table that holds the addresses is called a *jump table*.

Example 5–12 illustrates a jump table that serves five different users in a multiterminal computer system. This procedure, *SEL_USR*, interprets the contents of AL as a user identification code, and employs this code to call one of five user service procedures.

SEL_USR checks whether the entered code is valid, and jumps to an error-printing routine if the code is greater than four. SEL_USR converts a valid code to an index, then uses that index to perform an indirect jump to the appropriate user service procedure (USER0 through USER4). The user's RET instruction returns control to the program that called SEL_USR.

Example 5–12. A Multiuser Selection Procedure

```
; This procedure calls one of five user service
; procedures, based on a user indentification
; code in AL. The contents of DI are affected;
; AL is unaffected.
;
; This address table must be stored in the data
; segment.
;
U_ADDR DD USER0,USER1,USER2,USER3,USER4
;
; Here is the selection procedure.
;
SEL_USR    PROC    FAR
           CMP     AL,4              ;Invalid ID
                                     ; code?

           JA      U_ERROR
           MOV     DI,AL             ; No. Move ID
                                     ; code into DI
           SHL     DI,1              ; and convert
                                     ; it to an
                                     ; index
```

```
              SHL   DI,1
              JMP   FAR PTR U_ADDR[DI]  ;Jump to user
                                        ; procedure
     U_ERROR: ..          (Print an error message)
              ..
              RET
     SEL_USR  ENDP
```

5.5 Text Files

In the preceding sections we have been working with data structures that contain numbers. Word processing and other applications, however, involve manipulating non-numeric information—primarily text files.

Text files are lists whose elements are strings of ASCII characters. For instance, a text file that holds personnel information for a corporation will contain one element, or *record*, for each employee. In turn, each record has several sub-records, or *fields*, that list the employee's name, identification number, shift, pay rate, and so on. The 8086's string instructions are particularly convenient for manipulating text files.

You can manipulate text files with the same basic techniques you used to manipulate numeric files. But because of their multirecord construction, the programs that operate on text files must be somewhat different that those that operate on simple byte or word lists.

For instance, searching a text file usually requires you to compare a *part* of each entry (perhaps just the name field) to the search value, rather than comparing the entire entry. Similarly, bubble-sorting a text file requires you to compare single fields of adjacent entries, but move *entire* entries whenever an exchange is required.

As a simple example of a text file operation, let's look at a program that sorts a list of names and telephone numbers. The first location in the list holds a 2-byte count of the name-and-number entries.

Each entry in the list is 42 bytes long, divided into three fields: a 15-byte surname, a 15-byte first name/initial, and a 12-byte phone number. Any unused bytes in a field are assumed to contain ASCII "blank" characters. Hence, a typical entry in the list look like this:

```
   DB  'CORNELL',8 DUP (' ')
   DB  'RAY',12 DUP (' ')
   DB  '728-732-8437'
```

(Of course, you normally build text files by typing them in from the keyboard. For now, let's just assume the files are already in memory.)

Example 5–13 shows a procedure (PHONE_NOS) that bubble-sorts a telephone list stored in the extra segment. Its construction is similar to that of the "better bubble sort" procedure in Example 5–5.

After saving affected registers on the stack, the procedure reads the entry count and the address of the first entry into two variables, SAVE_CNT and FIRST_ENT. The instructions between NEXT and

SWAPEM set up and execute a CMPS operation. Here, DI points to an entry's surname field and SI points to the next entry's surname field, where these fields lie 42 bytes apart in memory.

The loop at SWAPEM exchanges two entries when needed. Since the entries are 42 bytes long, loop counter CX is initialized to 42. The remainder of the procedure is similar to Example 5–5.

Note that PHONE_NOS does not account for duplicate surnames. Upon finding a duplicate surname, the procedure *should* look at the first name fields of those entries and perform a second, alphabetical sort to put them in order. You might like to modify Example 5–13 to do this.

Example 5–13. Sort a Telephone List

```
; This procedure sorts a telephone list
; alphabetically. The list is composed of a word
; that holds a count of the entries, followed by
; the individual entries. Each entry is 42 bytes
; long, and divided into three fields: a 15-byte
; surname, a 15-byte first name/initial, and a
; 12-byte phone number. The list is in the extra
; segment, and its starting address (the address
; of the count word) is in DI.
;
; Set up these variables in the data segment.
;
FIRST_ENT   DW    ?
SAVE_CNT    DW    ?
;
;  Here is the main procedure.
;
PHONE_NOS   PROC
            PUSH    AX              ;Save scratch
                                    ; registers on
                                    ; stack

            PUSH    BX
            PUSH    CX
            PUSH    BP
            PUSH    DI
            PUSH    SI
            PUSH    DS
            CLD                     ;Set (DF) = 0,
                                    ; to move
                                    ; forward
            MOV     CX,ES:[DI]      ;Fetch entry
                                    ; count
            MOV     SAVE_CNT,CX     ; and save
                                    ; this value
                                    ; in memory
            ADD     DI,2            ;Get address
                                    ; of first
                                    ; entry
```

```
          MOV     FIRST_ENT,DI      ; and this
                                    ; address in
                                    ; memory
INIT:     MOV     BX,1              ;Exchange flag
                                    ; (BX) = 1
          DEC     SAVE_CNT          ;Get ready for
                                    ; count-1
                                    ; compares
          JZ      SORTED            ;Exit if SAVE_
                                    ; CNT is 0
          MOV     CX,SAVE_CNT       ;Load compare
                                    ; count into
                                    ; CX
          MOV     BP,FIRST_ENT      ; and first
                                    ; entry
                                    ; address into
                                    ; BP
NEXT:     MOV     DI,BP             ;Address one
                                    ; entry with
                                    ; DI
          MOV     SI,BP             ; and the next
                                    ; entry with
                                    ; SI
          ADD     SI,42
          PUSH    CX                ;Save current
                                    ; compare
                                    ; count
          MOV     CX,15             ;Compare 15-
                                    ; byte surname
                                    ; fields
                                    ;Is next
                                    ; surname <
                                    ; this
                                    ; surname?
REPE      CMPS    ES:BYTE PTR[SI]   ; ES:[DI]
          JAE     CONT              ; No. Check
                                    ; next pair
          MOV     CX,42             ; Yes.
                                    ; Exchange
                                    ; these
                                    ; entries
SWAPEM:   MOV     AL,ES:[BP]
          XCHG    ES:[BP+42],AL
          MOV     ES:[BP],AL
          INC     BP
          LOOP    SWAPEM
          SUB     BX,BX             ;Set exchange
                                    ; flag = 0
CONT:     POP     CX                ;Reload
                                    ; compare
                                    ; count
          ADD     BP,42             ;Point to next
                                    ; entry
```

```
                LOOP    NEXT        ; and compare
                                    ; next two
                                    ; names
                CMP     BX,0        ;Were any
                                    ; exchanges
                                    ; made?
                JE      INIT        ;  If so, make
                                    ; another pass
SORTED:         POP     DS          ;  If not,
                                    ; restore
                                    ; registers
                POP     SI
                POP     DI
                POP     BP
                POP     CX
                POP     BX
                POP     AX
                RET                 ;  and exit
PHONE_NOS       ENDP
```

Exercises (answers on page 208)

1. The list-processing procedures in this chapter don't check whether the list is empty (it has a count—which contains 0—but no data elements) before conducting an add, delete, or search operation. To rectify the situation, modify Example 5–1 so that AX becomes the first data element in a list if the list is empty. You can then use the modified procedure to build *new* lists, as well as to add elements to existing lists.
2. Write a procedure that searches an ordered list for the value in AX and, if the value is found, *replaces* the contents of the matching element with the value in BX.

6

Code Conversion

If you use an "electronic spreadsheet" or some other ready-made program that accepts numbers from the keyboard, the program automatically converts your keystrokes to binary numbers the microprocessor can operate on. It also converts results to digits it displays on the screen. If, however, you write assembly language programs that interact with the keyboard or the screen, you must build conversion routines into them. This chapter shows you how to convert keyboard keystrokes into binary numbers and binary results into display screen characters.

Since this is a general-purpose book, we can't know how your particular computer interacts with the keyboard or the screen. Therefore, we will just assume that it has some sort of "read-key" procedure, which we will call *READ_KEY*, and a "display-character" procedure, which we will call *DISP_CHAR*. Specifically, we will define READ_KEY as a procedure that reads a key value into AL and DISP_CHAR as a procedure that displays the character in AL on the screen, then advances the cursor. Many computers provide these procedures as interrupt service routines that you can call with INT instructions.

ASCII

In every computer system, there must be a way of communicating digital information between the processor and external devices. That is, there must be a way to *input* data from a keyboard or disk and *output* it to a printer, disk, or display screen.

The data must, of course, be in a form that is recognizable to the recipient—the peripheral device or the processor. In today's computers, most data is coded in a special form called *ASCII* (for American Standard Code for Information Interchange). Keyboards and other input devices are designed to send ASCII characters to the processor, and display screens and other output devices are designed to accept ASCII characters from it. ASCII characters are 8 bits long, but in this book we will assume that the leftmost bit (7) is always 0. Appendix A summarizes the complete ASCII character set.

6.1 Keyboard-Reading Procedure

In most cases, you will want to read a series of keyboard characters into the computer's memory—perhaps a name, a command word, or a number. Example 6–1 shows a procedure that reads key strokes from the keyboard and puts their ASCII codes into a buffer (KEY_CHAR) in the data segment. This procedure, READ_LINE, accepts key strokes until the operator presses Return or enters 30 keys. READ_LINE returns the buffer's starting address in BX and the character count in CX.

Example 6–1. Read Keyboard Characters into Memory

```
; This procedure reads keyboard characters into
; a buffer in memory until the operator presses
; Return or 30 keys have been entered. Upon
; return, the buffer's starting address is in BX
; and the character count is in CX.
; Only BX and CX are affected.
;
; Set up this buffer in the data segment.
;
KEY_CHARS  DB  30 DUP(?)
;
;  Here is the procedure.
;
READ_LINE PROC
          PUSH AX                 ;Save scratch
                                  ; registers
          PUSH DI
          MOV  DI,0               ;To start, key
                                  ; count is 0
          MOV  CX,30              ;Get ready for
                                  ; 30 key
                                  ; strokes
GET_KEY:  CALL READ_KEY          ;Read the next
                                  ; key
          CMP  AL,0DH             ;Is it a
                                  ; Carriage
                                  ; Return?
          JE   SAVE_CNT           ; If so, exit
          MOV  KEY_CHARS[DI],AL   ; Otherwise,
                                  ; store the
                                  ; code
```

```
                INC    DI              ; and update
                                       ; the key count
                LOOP   GET_KEY         ;Get next key
SAVE_CNT:       MOV    CX,DI           ;Final key
                                       ; count is in
                                       ; CX
                LEA    BX,KEY_CHARS    ;Buffer address
                                       ; is in BX
                POP    DI              ;Restore
                                       ; registers
                POP    AX
                RET                    ; and exit
READ_LINE ENDP
```

From now on, we will assume that you have used a procedure like READ _LINE to get a number into memory. Now you need to know how to convert this number (an ASCII string) into binary form, so the 8086 can operate on it.

6.2 Converting an ASCII String to Binary

Table 6–1 shows the ASCII codes for the decimal digits 0 through 9 and their binary equivalents (shown in hexadecimal). As you can see, the only ASCII values that interest us here are those that lie between 30H and 39H. You should also note that the binary equivalent of a decimal digit is nothing more than the four least-significant bits of the ASCII code.

As we've said before, decimal numbers can be expressed as a series

Table 6–1. The ASCII-based decimal characters.

ASCII Value (Hexadecimal)	Binary Value (Hexadecimal)
30	0
31	1
32	2
33	3
34	4
35	5
36	6
37	7
38	8
39	9

of digits multiplied by powers of 10. For example:

237 = (7 × 1) + (3 × 10) + (2 × 100)

or

237 = (7 × 10^0) + (3 × 10^1) + (2 × 10^2)

Since you enter digits of a number one at a time, a conversion routine from ASCII-based decimal to binary must include a multiply-by-10 operation. For instance, if the operator types in 93, the 9 must be multiplied by 10 before the 3 is added. In general, the conversion proceeds in this order:

- For the first (most-significant) digit, the conversion routine must convert the digit to binary, by stripping off the four high-order bits of the ASCII code, and store the binary value as a partial result.
- For all remaining digits, the conversion routine must convert the digit to binary, multiply the previous partial result by 10, then add the new digit to the product (thereby updating the partial result).

An ASCII-to-Binary Conversion Algorithm

You generally need to convert negative as well as positive numbers, and that number often includes a decimal point, so our conversion program must account for those characters, too. Figure 6–1 is a flowchart for an algorithm to convert an ASCII string in memory into a twos-complement (signed) binary number. We assume that the number fits into 16 bits, so its limits are −32768 and +32767.

At the beginning of this algorithm, the result and decimal count (number of digits to the right of the decimal point) are set to zero, and the program scans past any leading blanks. At this point, the program takes either of two paths: one for negative numbers, the other for positive numbers.

Both paths are nearly identical, except that a converted negative number is checked against −32,768 and must be complemented, whereas a positive number is checked against 32,767. The actual conversion is made by a procedure called CONV_AB, which is flowcharted in Figure 6–1A.

The CONV_AB procedure begins by checking whether the next string character is a decimal point. If it is, CONV_AB records the remaining character count as the decimal count, then advances the string pointer. If the next character is not a decimal point, CONV_AB checks whether it is a decimal digit. If this character is not a digit, CONV_AB declares it "invalid" and sets an error indicator, then returns to the main program.

Upon finding a valid digit character, CONV_AB multiplies the current partial result by 10, then converts the ASCII character to a digit and

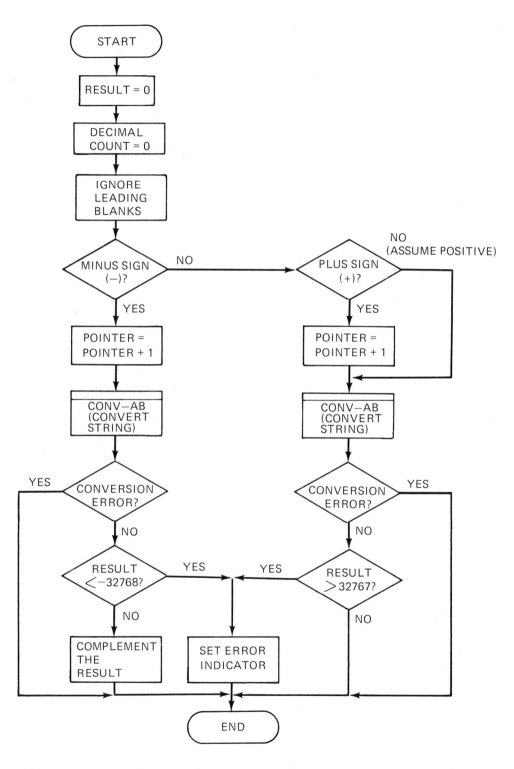

Figure 6–1. Algorithm to convert an ASCII
string to binary.

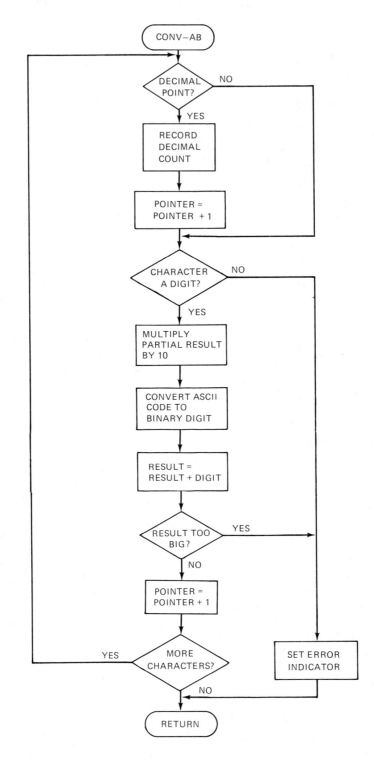

Figure 6–1A. Procedure called by ASCII conversion algorithms.

adds it to the result. If the addition produces a carry, CONV_AB sets the error indicator and returns. Otherwise, it increments the pointer and returns to the decimal point-checking instructions. When the entire string has been converted, CONV_AB returns to the main program.

The ASCII-to-Binary Conversion Program

Example 6–2 shows a procedure that implements the preceding algorithm. This procedure (ASCII_BIN) converts an ASCII string in the data segment—perhaps one entered with the READ_LINE procedure, as in Example 6–1—into a 16-bit signed number.

ASCII_BIN requires the starting address of the string to be in BX and the character count (7 maximum) to be in CX. By no coincidence, these are the parameters returned by READ_LINE. ASCII_BIN returns the 16-bit value in AX, the number of digits after the decimal point (if any) in DX, and the address of the first nonconvertible character in DI.

The value in DX indicates the magnitude of the result, and thereby tells you what *scale factor* to apply if you are operating on converted numbers of mixed sizes. The contents of DX can range from 0 (the result is an integer) to 5 (the result is a pure fraction). This means that if AX contains 1000H (decimal 4096) and DX contains 2, your result represents the decimal value 40.96.

If you wish to add this value to a previous result that returned DX equal to 3, you must first divide the previous result by 10. Similarly, if you wish to add 40.96 to a previous result that returned DX equal to 0, you must first divide the new result by 100.

Example 6–2. Convert an ASCII-Based Decimal Number to Binary

```
; This procedure converts an ASCII string in the
; data segment to its 16-bit, twos-complement
; binary equivalent.
; Upon entry, the starting address of the string
; must be in BX and the character count must be
; in CX. Upon return, the 16-bit value is in AX,
; a count of the number of digits after the
; decimal point is in DX, and the address of the
; first nonconvertible character is in DI.
; If the string contains more than seven
; characters, or the number is out of range
; (greater than 32,767 or less than -32,768), or
; the string contains a nonconvertible
; character, the Carry Flag (CF) is set to 1. If
; the conversion was made without error, CF is 0
; and DI contains 0FFH.
; The contents of BX and CX are unaffected.
```

```
;
ASCII_BIN  PROC
           PUSH  BX                        ;Save BX and
                                           ; CX
           PUSH  CX
           SUB   AX,AX                     ;To start,
                                           ; result = 0,
           SUB   DX,DX                      ; decimal
                                           ; count = 0,
           MOV   DI,0FFH                   ; assume no
                                           ; bad
                                           ; characters
           CMP   CX,7                      ;String too
                                           ; long?
           JA    NO_GOOD                   ; If so, set
                                           ; CF and exit
BLANKS:    CMP   BYTE PTR [BX],' '         ;Scan past
                                           ; leading
                                           ; blanks
           JNE   CHK_NEG
           INC   BX
           LOOP  BLANKS
CHK_NEG:   CMP   BYTE PTR [BX],'-'         ;Negative
                                           ; number?
           JNE   CHK_POS
           INC   BX                        ; If so,
                                           ; increment
                                           ; pointer,
           DEC   CX                        ; decrement
                                           ;   the count,
           CALL  CONV_B                    ; and convert
                                           ;   the string
           JC    THRU
           CMP   AX,32768                  ;Is the number
                                           ; too small?
           JA    NO_GOOD
           NEG   AX                        ; No.
                                           ; Complement
                                           ; the result
           JS    GOOD
CHK_POS:   CMP   BYTE PTR [BX],'+'         ;Positive
                                           ; number?
           JNE   GO_CONV
           INC   BX                        ; If so,
                                           ; increment
                                           ; pointer,
           DEC   CX                        ; decrement
                                           ;   the count,
GO_CONV:   CALL  CONV_AB                   ; and convert
                                           ;   the string
           JC    THRU
```

```
                CMP     AX,32767            ;Is the number
                                            ; too big?
                JA      NO_GOOD
GOOD:           CLC
                JNC     THRU
NO_GOOD:        STC                         ; If so, set
                                            ; Carry Flag
THRU:           POP     CX                  ;Restore
                                            ; registers
                POP     BX
                RET                         ; and exit
ASCII_BIN       ENDP
;
;  This procedure performs the actual conversion.
;
CONV_AB         PROC
                PUSH    BP                  ;Save scratch
                                            ; registers
                PUSH    BX
                PUSH    SI
CHK_PT:         CMP     DX,0                ;Decimal point
                                            ; already
                                            ; found?
                JNZ     RANGE               ; If so, skip
                                            ; following
                                            ; check
                CMP     BYTE PTR DS:        ;Decimal
                          [BP],'.'          ; point?
                JNE     RANGE
                DEC     CX                  ; If so,
                                            ; decrement
                                            ; count
                MOV     DX,CX               ; and record
                                            ; it in DX
                JZ      END_CONV            ; Exit if CX =
                                            ; 0
                INC     BP                  ; Increment
                                            ; pointer
RANGE:          CMP     BYTE PTR DS:        ;If the
                          [BP],'0'          ; character is
                                            ; not a
                JB      NON_DIG             ; digit...
                CMP     BYTE PTR DS:
                          [BP],'9'
                JBE     DIGIT
NON_DIG:        MOV     DI,BP               ; put its
                                            ; address in
                                            ; DI,
                STC                         ; set the
                                            ; Carry Flag,
                JC      END_CONV            ; and exit
```

```
DIGIT:       MOV    SI,10             ;The character
                                      ; is a digit,
             PUSH   DX
             MUL    SI                ; so multiply
                                      ; AX by 10
             POP    DX
             MOV    BL,DS:[BP]        ; Fetch ASCII
                                      ; code,
             AND    BX,0FH            ; save only
                                      ; high bits,
             ADD    AX,BX             ; and update
                                      ; partial
                                      ; result
             JC     END_CONV          ; Exit if
                                      ; result is
                                      ; too big
             INC    BP                ; Otherwise,
                                      ; increment BP
             LOOP   CHK_PT            ; and continue
             CLC                      ;When done,
                                      ; clear Carry
                                      ; Flag
END_CONV:    POP    SI                ;Restore
                                      ; registers
             POP    BX
             POP    BP
             RET                      ; and return
                                      ; to caller
CONV_AB      ENDP
```

The Carry Flag (CF) tells you whether an error occurred during the conversion operation. If CF is 0, the results are valid, but if CF is 1, ASCII _BIN detected one of the following errors:

- If the string was longer than seven characters (CX > 7), AX and DX holds 0 and DI holds 00FFH.
- If an invalid character was found, DI holds its offset value.
- If a number was out-of-range (more negative than −32768 or more positive than 32767), AX is nonzero and DI holds 00FFH.

To check the validity of the answer, you should call ASCII_BIN in this context:

```
             CALL   ASCII_BIN         ;Call the conversion
                                      ; procedure
             JNC    VALID             ;Is the answer
                                      ; valid?
             OR     DI,DI             ; No. Find the error
                                      ; condition
             JNZ    INV_CHAR
             OR     AX,AX
```

```
          JNZ     RANGE_ER
          ..                      ;  String was too
                                  ;    long
          ..
RANGE_ER: ..                      ;  Number out-of-
                                  ;    range
          ..
INV_CHAR: ..                      ;  Invalid character
          ..
VALID:    ..                      ;The answer is valid
          ..
```

6.3 Converting a Binary Number to ASCII

If you want to print a result or display it on the screen, you must first convert the result to ASCII. Fortunately, this is easy to do. To convert a 16-bit binary number to ASCII, you need a program that determines how many 1s, 10s, 100s, 1,000s, and 10,000s the number contains, and converts each of those counts into an ASCII character. You can either output the ASCII characters as they are calculated or store them in memory as a string and output them later with another program.

Example 6–3 shows a procedure (BIN_ASCII) that converts a 16-bit binary number in AX to an ASCII string in memory. To derive the various counts, BIN_ASCII successively divides the contents of AX by 10, then uses the remainder of each divide operation to build the string. BIN_ASCII returns the address of the converted string in BX and the character count in CX.

Once BIN_ASCII has formed the ASCII display string, you can send the number to the screen, digit-by-digit, with this kind of sequence:

```
          MOV     SI,BX
          CLD                     ;Move forward in
                                  ; string
NEXT_DIG: LODSB                   ;Fetch next digit
          CALL    DISP_CHAR       ; and display it
          LOOP    NEXT_DIG
```

Example 6–3. Convert a Binary Number to an ASCII String

```
; This procedure converts a signed binary number
; to a 6-byte ASCII string (sign plus five
; digits) in the data segment. Upon entry, the
; number to be converted must be in AX and the
; starting address of the memory buffer must be
; in BX. Upon return, BX holds the address of
; the converted output string and CX holds the
```

```
; length of the string. Other registers are
; preserved.
;
BIN_ASCII    PROC
             PUSH    DX              ;Save affected
                                     ; registers
             PUSH    SI
             PUSH    AX              ;Save binary value
             MOV     CX,6            ;Fill buffer with
                                     ; spaces
FILL_BUFF:   MOV     BYTE PTR [BX],' '
             INC     BX
             LOOP    FILL_BUFF
             MOV     SI,10           ;Get ready to divide
                                     ; by 10
             OR      AX,AX           ;If value is
                                     ; negative,
             JNS     CLR_DVD
             NEG     AX              ; make it positive
CLR_DVD:     SUB     DX,DX           ;Clear upper half of
                                     ; dividend
             DIV     SI              ;Divide AX by 10
             ADD     DX,'0'          ;Convert remainder to
                                     ; ASCII digit
             DEC     BX              ;Back up through
                                     ; buffer
             MOV     [BX],DL         ;Store this character
                                     ; in the string
             INC     CX              ;Count converted
                                     ; character
             OR      AX,AX           ;All done?
             JNZ     CLR_DVD         ; No. Get next digit
             POP     AX              ; Yes. Retrieve
                                     ; original value
             OR      AX,AX           ;Was it negative?
             JNS     NO_MORE
             DEC     BX              ; Yes. Store sign
             MOV     BYTE PTR [BX],'-'
             INC     CX              ;   and increase
                                     ; character count
NO_MORE:     POP     SI              ;Restore registers
             POP     DX
             RET                     ; and exit
BIN_ASCII    ENDP
```

7

The 8087 Numeric Data Processor

The 8087 Numeric Data Processor (NDP) is a chip that performs complex mathematical calculations. It is designed to be installed along with an 8086 or 8088 microprocessor to extend the original chip's instruction set and arithmetic capability. In fact, some computers (notably, the IBM Personal Computer and its "work-alikes") provide an extra socket for an 8087.

As you know, the 8086 itself can do arithmetic, but its instruction set can operate only on five-digit (2-byte) integers, and you only get the four basic functions: add, subtract, multiply, and divide. The 8087, however, can perform a wide variety of arithmetic and transcendental operations (logarithms and trigonometric functions) on integer and real numbers as large as 18 digits (10 bytes). And because the 8087's instructions are built into hardware, it can produce a dramatic improvement over doing these operations with 8086 instructions. For example, it might take 2,100 μs to do a 64-bit multiplication with an 8086 program, but an 8087 can do the same job in 30 μs!

The 8087 is referred to as a *coprocessor*, because it acts in combination with the main processor (the 8086 or 8088) to execute your programs. When you run a program with software that is designed to use the 8087, the 8086 executes the instructions that it recognizes and the 8087 executes those that *it* recognizes. In other words, an 8086/8087 pair operates as though it were a single super processor.

If your program is written in a high-level language such as BASIC or Pascal, it will use the 8087 automatically. If it is written in assembly language, you can either insert 8087 instructions with the 8086's ESC (escape) instruction or buy an assembler that recognizes the 8087 instruction set.

This chapter gives you a brief overview of the 8087 NDP. For full details, order a copy of Richard Startz' excellent book *8087 Applications and Programming* (Robert J. Brady Co., 1983).

7.1 Internal Registers

The 8087 has eight, 80-bit data registers, plus a status word and a control word, both 16 bits long. The status word is similar to the 8086's flags register. The control word governs the way the 8087 handles rounding, infinity, and precision. Its precision bits let you specify whether results should have 64, 53, or 24 bits of precision; 64 bits is the default, the others are provided to produce results that are compatible with previous floating-point packages.

Working with the 8087's data registers is quite different than working with the 8086's registers, in that you generally don't address them individually. Instead, you use them as a stack.

The 8087's Stack

You will recall that the 8086 uses a stack to hold return information during procedure calls and interrupt servicing, and that we can use it to preserve the contents of registers. A stack operates like a plate dispenser in a cafeteria; the last item you put on the stack is the first one you can remove from it. The 8087's data registers work in the same way. That is, you always put numbers into the top register, and when you do, it pushes the rest of the registers "down" one position in the stack. (As with the 8086, the 8087 does not actually move the registers, it just changes the contents of a "stack pointer.")

Because the data registers operate as a stack, most of the 8087's instructions use the stack contents implicitly. For example, when you give the 8087 an add instruction, it adds the contents of two numbers on the stack and leaves the result on the stack. If you have programmed in a stack-oriented language such as Forth, you will feel quite comfortable programming the 8087; otherwise, it will probably take you some time to get used to this concept.

Floating-Point Format

The data registers hold numbers in "floating-point" format, the computer's version of scientific notation. In this notation, you would write -150 as

$$-1.5 \times 10^2$$

The 8087's data registers represent such numbers by splitting them into three fields: a 1-bit sign, a 15-bit exponent, and a 64-bit significand (or *mantissa*). Hence, a data register would store −150 with 1 in the sign field, 2 in the exponent field, and 15 in the significand field.

Fortunately, we rarely need to be concerned about how the 8087 stores numbers. What we *do* need to know is what kinds of data it can operate on.

7.2 Data Types

The 8087 can operate on seven types of data: three types of integers (word, short, and long), three types of reals (short, long, and temporary), and packed decimal. Table 7–1 summarizes the data types.

Of the integer types, the four-digit *word integer*, which corresponds to BASIC's integer data type, is useful for indexing arrays and other data structures. Since a word integer can hold values ranging from −32,768 to 32,767, you probably won't find many applications for the short and long integer types.

Short real and *long real* correspond to BASIC's single- and double-precision data types, respectively. Short real numbers are accurate to about seven decimal places. This means that numbers that differ only in the eighth place will appear to the 8087 to be the same number. (For example, 1.23456789 and 1.12345681 would be considered equal.) Hence, short real numbers are convenient for storing input data, but any calculating you do should be performed with long real numbers, to minimize the effect of round-offs. Long real numbers are accurate to about 16 places.

Temporary real is the format in which the 8087 stores numbers in its data registers. Since this format uses a 64-bit significand, every other data type will fit into it without loss of precision. With its 80-bit length, the temporary real format shields the user from cumulative rounding errors and underflow or overflow in intermediate calculations.

Finally, *packed decimal* is used for business and data processing. It can hold up to 18 significant digits, where the digits are "packed" two to a

Table 7–1. 8087 data types.

Data Type	Bits	Significant Digits	Range
Word integer	16	4	−32,768 to 32,767
Short integer	32	9	-2×10^9 to 2×10^9
Long integer	64	18	-9×10^{18} to 9×10^{18}
Short real	32	6 or 7	10^{-37} to 10^{38}
Long real	64	15 or 16	10^{-307} to 10^{308}
Temporary real	80	19	10^{-4932} to 10^{4932}
Packed decimal	80	18	18 decimal digits + sign

byte in memory. You will recall this approach from our discussion of binary-coded decimal (BCD) numbers in Chapter 3.

7.3 Instruction Set

The 8087's instruction set may be divided into six groups: data transfer, arithmetic, comparison, transcendental, constants, and control. Table 7–2 gives their mnemonics, a short description, and the typical execution

Table 7–2. 8087 instruction set.

Mnemonic	Description	Time (μs)
Data Transfer		
FBLB	Load packed decimal	69
FBSTP	Store and pop packed decimal	117
FILD	Load integer	12
FIST	Store integer	21
FISTP	Store and pop integer	21
FLD	Load real	13
FST	Store real	23
FSTP	Store real and pop	23
FXCH	Exchange registers	3
Arithmetic		
FADD	Add real	18
FADDP	Add real and pop	18
FIADD	Add integer	27
FSUB	Subtract real	18
FSUBP	Subtract real and pop	18
FISUB	Subtract integer	27
FSUBR	Subtract real reversed	18
FSUBRP	Subtract real reversed and pop	18
FISUBR	Subtract integer reversed	27
FMUL	Multiply real	28
FMULP	Multiply real and pop	28
FIMUL	Multiply integer	28
FDIV	Divide real	41
FDIVP	Divide real and pop	41
FIDIV	Divide integer	49
FDIVR	Divide real reversed	41
FDIVRP	Divide real reversed and pop	41
FIDIVR	Divide integer reversed	49
FSQRT	Square root	37
FSCALE	Scale by a power of two	7
FPREM	Partial remainder	25
FRNDINT	Round to integer	9

Table 7-2. 8087 instruction set (continued).

Mnemonic	Description	Time (μs)
EXTRACT	Extract exponent and significand	10
FABS	Absolute value	3
FCHS	Change sign	3

Comparison

FCOM	Compare real	9
FCOMP	Compare real and pop	10
FCOMPP	Compare real and pop twice	10
FICOM	Compare integer	19
FICOMP	Compare integer and pop	19
FTST	Test top of stack for zero	9
FXAM	Examine top of stack	4

Transcendental

F2XM1	2 to the X, minus 1	100
FYL2X	Y times $\log_2 X$	190
FYL2XP1	Y times $\log_2 (X+1)$	170
FPTAN	Partial tangent	90
FPATAN	Partial arctangent	130

Constants

FLDZ	Load zero	3
FLD1	Load one	4
FLDPI	Load pi	4
FLDL2T	Load $\log_2 10$	4
FLDL2E	Load $\log_2 e$	4
FLDLG2	Load common logarithm of 2	4
FLDLN2	Load natural logarithm of 2	4

Control

FLDCW	Load control word	4
FSTCW	Store control word	5
FSTSW	Store status word	5
FSAVE	Save state	44
FRSTOR	Restore state	44
FLDENV	Load environment	10
FSTENV	Store environment	11
FWAIT	Wait (halt the 8088)	—
FINIT	Initialize (reset) the 8087	1
FENI	Enable interrupts	1
FDISI	Disable interrupts	1
FCLEX	Clear exceptions	1
FINCSTP	Increment stack pointer	2
FDECSTP	Decrement stack pointer	2
FFREE	Free (clear) register	2
FNOP	No operation	3

times (in microseconds) with a 5-MHz 8087. The times are taken from Richard Startz' book, which we mentioned earlier.

The *data transfer* instructions move numbers to and from the top of the 8087's data register stack.

The *arithmetic* instructions provide the four basic operations (add, subtract, multiply, and divide), plus other convenient functions such as square root and absolute value. The subtract and divide instructions come in two forms. With the standard forms, you subtract a source from a destination or divide a destination by a source. With the "reversed" forms, you subtract a destination from a source or divide a source by a destination. The reversed forms let you leave results in memory, which may only be a source operand.

The *comparison* instructions compare the top number on the stack to another stack number or a memory location. Compares are convenient for finding the largest number in an array or determining whether a number is less than, equal to, or greater than zero.

The *transcendental* instructions compute logarithms and trigonometric functions. Athough the 8087 provides only tangent and arctangent instructions, it is fairly easy to derive other trigonometric functions from them.

The *constant* instructions push any of seven constants onto the stack: zero, one, pi, or four logarithmic values. In all cases, the 8087 gives them full temporary real (19-digit) accuracy.

The *control* instructions let you preserve status information, change the way the 8087 rounds results, enable and disable interrupts, and do a variety of other "housekeeping" jobs. One instruction, FWAIT, generates an 8086 WAIT instruction, which prevents it from accessing a memory location that the 8087 is using.

7.4 Summary

The 8087 Numeric Data Processor (NDP) is a powerful device that can dramatically improve your computer's ability to perform mathematical calculations. It accepts seven different types of data—three integer, three real, and packed decimal—giving maximum flexibility for any kind of calculation you need. No matter what data type you use, the 8087 performs all internal calculations using an 80-bit floating-point format, which gives accuracy to 19 significant places. This means not only that your answers will be highly precise, but also that you will rarely encounter overflow or underflow errors.

The 8087 provides instructions for adding, subtracting, multiplying, and dividing both integer and real numbers. It also has a variety of logarithmic and trigonometric instructions, plus special ones that perform tasks you frequently need, such as extracting a square root and finding an absolute value. The slowest instruction takes 190 μs to execute and the fastest takes just 1 μs, but most require from 18 to 40 μs.

Programming the 8087 in assembly language may take some getting used to, because it has a stack-oriented architecture. The short time it takes to accustom yourself, however, more than makes up for the agony you would have to endure in writing multiprecision arithmetic procedures for the 8086.

Hexadecimal/Decimal Conversion

HEXADECIMAL COLUMNS											
6		**5**		**4**		**3**		**2**		**1**	
HEX	DEC	HEX	DEC	HEX	DEC	HEX	DEC	HEX	DEC	HEX	DEC
0	0	0	0	0	0	0	0	0	0	0	0
1	1,048,576	1	65,536	1	4,096	1	256	1	16	1	1
2	2,097,152	2	131,072	2	8,192	2	512	2	32	2	2
3	3,145,728	3	196,608	3	12,288	3	768	3	48	3	3
4	4,194,304	4	262,144	4	16,384	4	1,024	4	64	4	4
5	5,242,880	5	327,680	5	20,480	5	1,280	5	80	5	5
6	6,291,456	6	393,216	6	24,576	6	1,536	6	96	6	6
7	7,340,032	7	458,752	7	28,672	7	1,792	7	112	7	7
8	8,388,608	8	524,288	8	32,768	8	2,048	8	128	8	8
9	9,437,184	9	589,824	9	36,864	9	2,304	9	144	9	9
A	10,485,760	A	655,360	A	40,960	A	2,560	A	160	A	10
B	11,534,336	B	720,896	B	45,056	B	2,816	B	176	B	11
C	12,582,912	C	786,432	C	49,152	C	3,072	C	192	C	12
D	13,631,488	D	851,968	D	53,248	D	3,328	D	208	D	13
E	14,680,064	E	917,504	E	57,344	E	3,584	E	224	E	14
F	15,728,640	F	983,040	F	61,440	F	3,840	F	240	F	15
7654		3210		7654		3210		7654		3210	
Byte				Byte				Byte			

POWERS OF 2

2^n	n
256	8
512	9
1 024	10
2 048	11
4 096	12
8 192	13
16 384	14
32 768	15
65 536	16
131 072	17
262 144	18
524 288	19
1 048 576	20
2 097 152	21
4 194 304	22
8 388 608	23
16 777 216	24

$2^0 = 16^0$
$2^4 = 16^1$
$2^8 = 16^2$
$2^{12} = 16^3$
$2^{16} = 16^4$
$2^{20} = 16^5$
$2^{24} = 16^6$
$2^{28} = 16^7$
$2^{32} = 16^8$
$2^{36} = 16^9$
$2^{40} = 16^{10}$
$2^{44} = 16^{11}$
$2^{48} = 16^{12}$
$2^{52} = 16^{13}$
$2^{56} = 16^{14}$
$2^{60} = 16^{15}$

POWERS OF 16

16^n	n
1	0
16	1
256	2
4 096	3
65 536	4
1 048 576	5
16 777 216	6
268 435 456	7
4 294 967 296	8
68 719 476 736	9
1 099 511 627 776	10
17 592 186 044 416	11
281 474 976 710 656	12
4 503 599 627 370 496	13
72 057 594 037 927 936	14
1 152 921 504 606 846 976	15

Figure A–1. Hexadecimal/decimal conversion.

B

ASCII Character Set

LSD \ MSD		0 000	1 001	2 010	3 011	4 100	5 101	6 110	7 111
0	0000	NUL	DLE	SP	0	@	P		p
1	0001	SOH	DC1	!	1	A	Q	a	q
2	0010	STX	DC2	"	2	B	R	b	r
3	0011	ETX	DC3	#	3	C	S	c	s
4	0100	EOT	DC4	$	4	D	T	d	t
5	0101	ENQ	NAK	%	5	E	U	e	u
6	0110	ACK	SYN	&	6	F	V	f	v
7	0111	BEL	ETB	'	7	G	W	g	w
8	1000	BS	CAN	(	8	H	X	h	x
9	1001	HT	EM	)	9	I	Y	i	y
A	1010	LF	SUB	*	:	J	Z	j	z
B	1011	VT	ESC	+	;	K	[	k	{
C	1100	FF	FS	,	<	L	\	l	|
D	1101	CR	GS	–	=	M	]	m	}
E	1110	SO	RS	•	>	N	↑	n	~
F	1111	SI	US	/	?	O	←	o	DEL

NUL — Null
SOH — Start of Heading
STX — Start of Text
ETX — End of Text
EOT — End of Transmission
ENQ — Enquiry
ACK — Acknowledge
BEL — Bell
BS — Backspace
HT — Horizontal Tabulation
LF — Line Feed
VT — Vertical Tabulation
FF — Form Feed
CR — Carriage Return
SO — Shift Out
SI — Shift In

DLE — Data Link Escape
DC — Device Control
NAK — Negative Acknowledge
SYN — Synchronous Idle
ETB — End of Transmission Block
CAN — Cancel
EM — End of Medium
SUB — Substitute
ESC — Escape
FS — File Separator
GS — Group Separator
RS — Record Separator
US — Unit Separator
SP — Space (Blank)
DEL — Delete

Figure B–1. ASCII character set.

C

8086/8088 Instruction Times

You can use the tables in this appendix to calculate how long the microprocessor will take to execute instructions in your program. These tables give execution times in *clock cycles*. To convert clock cycles to microseconds, divide by your computer's clock speed in megahertz. For example, if your computer has a 5-MHz clock, divide clock cycles by 5.

Table C–1 lists execution time increments for operand addressing modes that reference memory. You should add these increments to the execution times in Table C–2 that include "EA".

Table C–2 lists the number of clocks each instruction takes to execute and the number of bytes it occupies in memory. In the Clocks column, the number in parentheses is the cycle count you use if you are operating on 16-bit data with an 8088.

When using Table C–2, note the following:

1. Some instructions take more time to execute if its operands are word values, rather than byte values. For these instructions, execution times are listed in the form *b(w)*, where *b* denotes the number of clock cycles for byte operands and *w* denotes the number of clock cycles for word operands.
2. Most instructions that reference memory have the abbreviation EA in the Clocks column. This abbreviation tells you that additional clock cycles are required to calculate the Effective Address; these incremental times are listed in Table C–1.
3. The execution time of conditional jump instructions and loop instructions depends on whether the transfer is made. If the transfer *is* made, use the larger number in the Clocks column. Otherwise, if execution "drops through" to the next instruction, use the smaller number.

For instance, suppose you want to find the execution time of the instruction

```
ADD  SS:[BX],DX
```

This instruction has the general form *ADD memory, register*, so its execution time is given by the equation

```
16(24)+EA
```

Since this particular ADD instruction operates on word values, the execution time differs between the 8086 and 8088. If you have an 8086, use 16; if you have an 8088, use 24. Because the equation contains EA, you must also add an address calculation time from Table C–1. The destination operand has the form [BX], which tells you to add 5 additional clock cycles. Because this operand has a segment override, however, you must add 2 more clock cycles. Combining these three values gives the following execution times:

8086: Time = 16+5+2 = 23 clock cycles
8088: Time = 24+5+2 = 31 clock cycles

Table C–1. Effective address calculation time.

EA Components	Operand Formats	Clocks*
Displacement Only	disp label	6
Base or Index Only	[BX] [BP] [DI] [SI]	5
Displacement + Base or Index	[BX]+disp [BP]+disp [DI]+disp [SI]+disp	9
Base + Index	[BX] [SI] [BX] [DI]	7
	[BP] [SI] [BP] [DI]	8
Displacement + Base + Index	[BX] [SI]+disp [BX] [DI]+disp	11
	[BP] [SI]+disp [BP] [DI]+disp	12

*Add 2 clocks for segment override

Table C–2. Instruction times.

Instruction		Clocks	Bytes
AAA		4	1
AAD		60	2
AAM		83	2
AAS		4	1
ADC	register,register	3	2
ADC	register,memory	9(13) + EA	2–4
ADC	memory,register	16(24) + EA	2–4
ADC	register,immediate	4	3–4
ADC	memory,immediate	17(25) + EA	3–6
ADC	accumulator,immediate	4	2–3
ADD	register,register	3	2
ADD	register,memory	9(13) + EA	2–4
ADD	memory,register	16(24) + EA	2–4
ADD	register,immediate	4	3–4
ADD	memory,immediate	17(25) + EA	3–6
ADD	accumulator,immediate	4	2–3
AND	register,register	3	2
AND	register,memory	9(13) + EA	2–4
AND	memory,register	16(24) + EA	2–4
AND	register,immediate	4	3–6
AND	memory,immediate	17(15) + EA	3–6
AND	accumulator,immediate	4	2–3
CALL	near-proc	23	3
CALL	far-proc	36	5
CALL	memptr16	29	2–4
CALL	regptr16	24	2
CALL	memptr32	57	2–4
CBW		2	1
CLC		2	1
CLD		2	1
CLI		2	1
CMC		2	1
CMP	register,register	3	2
CMP	register,memory	9(13) + EA	2–4
CMP	memory,register	9(13) + EA	2–4
CMP	register,immediate	4	3–4
CMP	memory,immediate	10(14) + EA	3–6
CMP	accumulator,immediate	4	2–3
CMPS	dest-string,source-string	22(30)	1

Table C–2. Instruction times (continued).

Instruction		Clocks	Bytes
CMPS	(repeat) dest-string, source-string	9+22(30)/rep	1
CWD		5	1
DAA		4	1
DAS		4	1
DEC	reg16	2	1
DEC	reg8	3	2
DEC	memory	15(23)+EA	2–4
DIV	reg8	80–90	2
DIV	reg16	144–162	2
DIV	mem8	[86–96]+EA	2–4
DIV	mem16	[154–172]+EA	2–4
ESC	immediate,memory	8(35)+EA	2–4
ESC	immediate,register	2	2
HLT		2	1
IDIV	reg8	101–112	2
IDIV	reg16	165–184	2
IDIV	mem8	[107–118]+EA	2–4
IDIV	mem16	[175–194]+EA	2–4
IMUL	reg8	80–98	2
IMUL	reg16	128–154	2
IMUL	mem8	[86–104]+EA	2–4
IMUL	mem16	[138–164]+EA	2–4
IN	accumulator, immed8	10(14)	2
IN	accumulator, DX	8(12)	1
INC	reg16	2	1
INC	reg8	3	2
INC	memory	15(23)+EA	2–4
INT	3	52	1
INT	immed8 (not type 3)	51	2
INTO		53 or 4	1
IRET		32	1

All conditional jump instructions except JCXZ:

Jccc	short-label	16 or 4	2
JCXZ	short-label	18 or 6	2
JMP	short-label	15	2
JMP	near-label	15	3
JMP	far-label	15	5

Table C–2. Instruction times (continued).

Instruction		Clocks	Bytes
JMP	memptr16	18 + EA	2–4
JMP	regptr16	11	2
JMP	memptr32	24 + EA	2–4
LAHF		4	1
LDS	reg16,mem32	24 + EA	2–4
LEA	reg16,mem16	2 + EA	2–4
LES	reg16,mem32	24 + EA	2–4
LOCK		2	1
LODS	source-string	12(16)	1
LODS	(repeat) source-string	9 + 13(17)/rep	1
LOOP	short-label	17 or 5	2
LOOPE/ LOOPZ	short-label	18 or 6	2
LOOPNE/ LOOPNZ	short-label	19 or 5	2
MOV	memory,accumulator	10(14)	3
MOV	accumulator,memory	10(14)	3
MOV	register,register	2	2
MOV	register,memory	8(12) + EA	2–4
MOV	memory,register	9(13) + EA	2–4
MOV	register,immediate	4	2–3
MOV	memory,immediate	10(14) + EA	3–6
MOV	seg-reg,reg16	2	2
MOV	seg-reg,mem16	8(12) + EA	2–4
MOV	reg16,seg-reg	2	2
MOV	memory,seg-reg	9(13) + EA	2–4
MOVS	dest-string, source-string	18(26)	1
MOVS	(repeat) dest-string, source-string	9 + 17(25)/rep	1
MUL	reg8	70–77	2
MUL	reg16	118–133	2
MUL	mem8	[76–83] + EA	2–4
MUL	mem16	[128–143] + EA	2–4
NEG	register	3	2
NEG	memory	16(24) + EA	2–4
NOP		3	1
NOT	register	3	2
NOT	memory	16(24) + EA	2–4

Table C–2. Instruction times (continued).

Instruction		Clocks	Bytes
OR	register,register	3	2
OR	register,memory	9(13) + EA	2–4
OR	memory,register	16(24) + EA	2–4
OR	register,immediate	4	3–6
OR	memory,immediate	17(15) + EA	3–6
OR	accumulator,immediate	4	2–3
OUT	immed8,accumulator	10(14)	2
OUT	DX,accumulator	8(12)	1
POP	register	12	1
POP	seg-reg (CS illegal)	12	1
POP	memory	25 + EA	2–4
POPF		12	1
PUSH	register	15	1
PUSH	seg-reg (CS legal)	14	1
PUSH	memory	24 + EA	2–4
PUSHF		14	1
RCL	register,1	2	2
RCL	register,CL	8 + 4/bit	2
RCL	memory,1	15(23) + EA	2–4
RCL	memory,CL	20(28) + EA + 4/bit	2–4
RCR	register,1	2	2
RCR	register,CL	8 + 4/bit	2
RCR	memory,1	15(23) + EA	2–4
RCR	memory,CL	20(28) + EA + 4/bit	2–4
REP		2	1
REPE/REPZ		2	1
REPNE/REPNZ		2	1
RET	(intra-seg,no pop)	20	1
RET	(intra-seg,pop)	24	3
RET	(inter-seg,pop)	32	1
RET	(inter-seg,no pop)	31	3
ROL	register,1	2	2
ROL	register,CL	8 + 4/bit	2
ROL	memory,1	15(23) + EA	2–4
ROL	memory,CL	20(28) + EA + 4/bit	2–4
ROR	register,1	2	2
ROR	register,CL	8 + 4/bit	2
ROR	memory,1	15(23) + EA	2–4
ROR	memory,CL	20(28) + EA + 4/bit	2–4
SAHF		4	1

Table C–2. Instruction times (continued).

Instruction		Clocks	Bytes
SAL/SHL	register,1	2	2
SAL/SHL	register,CL	8 + 4/bit	2
SAL/SHL	memory,1	15(23) + EA	2–4
SAL/SHL	memory,CL	20(28) + EA + 4/bit	2–4
SAR	register,1	2	2
SAR	register,CL	8 + 4/bit	2
SAR	memory,1	15(23) + EA	2–4
SAR	memory,CL	20(28) + EA + 4/bit	2–4
SBB	register,register	3	2
SBB	register,memory	9(13) + EA	2–4
SBB	memory,register	16(24) + EA	2–4
SBB	register,immediate	4	3–4
SBB	memory,immediate	17(25) + EA	3–6
SBB	accumulator,immediate	4	2–3
SCAS	dest-string	15(19)	1
SCAS	(repeat) dest-string	9 + 15(19)/rep	1
SHR	register,1	2	2
SHR	register,CL	8 + 4/bit	2
SHR	memory,1	15(23) + EA	2–4
SHR	memory,CL	20(28) + EA + 4/bit	2–4
STC		2	1
STD		2	1
STI		2	1
STOS	dest-string	11(15)	1
STOS	(repeat) dest-string	9 + 10(14)/rep	1
SUB	register,register	3	2
SUB	register,memory	9(13) + EA	2–4
SUB	memory,register	16(24) + EA	2–4
SUB	register,immediate	4	3–4
SUB	memory,immediate	17(25) + EA	3–6
SUB	accumulator,immediate	4	2–3
TEST	register,register	3	2
TEST	register,memory	9(13) + EA	2–4
TEST	register,immediate	5	3–4
TEST	memory,immediate	11 + EA	3–6
TEST	accumulator,immediate	4	2–3
WAIT		3 + 5n	1
XCHG	accumulator,reg16	3	1
XCHG	memory,register	17(25) + EA	2–4
XCHG	register,register	4	2

Table C–2. Instruction times (continued).

Instruction		Clocks	Bytes
XLAT	source-table	11	1
XOR	register,register	3	2
XOR	register,memory	9(13) + EA	2–4
XOR	memory,register	16(24) + EA	2–4
XOR	register,immediate	4	3–6
XOR	memory,immediate	17(15) + EA	3–6
XOR	accumulator,immediate	4	2–3

D

8086/8088 Instruction Set Summary

Table D–1 summarizes the 8086/8088 instruction set in alphabetical order. For each instruction, it shows the general assembler format and which flags are affected. In the *Flags* column, — means unchanged, * means may have changed, and ? means undefined.

Table D–1. 8086/8088 instruction set.

Mnemonic	Assembler Format		OF	DF	IF	TF	SF	ZF	AF	PF	CF
							Flags				
AAA	AAA		?	—	—	—	?	?	*	?	*
AAD	AAD		?	—	—	—	*	*	?	*	?
AAM	AAM		?	—	—	—	*	*	?	*	?
AAS	AAS		?	—	—	—	?	?	*	?	*
ADC	ADC	destination,source	*	—	—	—	*	*	*	*	*
ADD	ADD	destination,source	*	—	—	—	*	*	*	*	*
AND	AND	destination,source	0	—	—	—	*	*	?	*	0
CALL	CALL	target	—	—	—	—	—	—	—	—	—
CBW	CBW		—	—	—	—	—	—	—	—	—
CLC	CLC		—	—	—	—	—	—	—	—	0
CLD	CLD		—	0	—	—	—	—	—	—	—
CLI	CLI		—	—	0	—	—	—	—	—	—
CMC	CMC		—	—	—	—	—	—	—	—	*
CMP	CMP	destination,source	*	—	—	—	*	*	*	*	*
CMPS	CMPS	dest-string,source-string	*	—	—	—	*	*	*	*	*
CMPSB	CMPSB		*	—	—	—	*	*	*	*	*
CMPSW	CMPSW		*	—	—	—	*	*	*	*	*

Table D–1. 8086/8088 instruction set (continued).

Mnemonic	Assembler Format		OF	DF	IF	TF	SF	ZF	AF	PF	CF
CWD	CWD		—	—	—	—	—	—	—	—	—
DAA	DAA		?	—	—	—	*	*	*	*	*
DAS	DAS		?	—	—	—	*	*	*	*	*
DEC	DEC	destination	*	—	—	—	*	*	*	*	—
DIV	DIV	source	?	—	—	—	?	?	?	?	?
ESC	ESC	ext-opcode,source	—	—	—	—	—	—	—	—	—
HLT	HLT		—	—	—	—	—	—	—	—	—
IDIV	IDIV	source	?	—	—	—	?	?	?	?	?
IMUL	IMUL	source	*	—	—	—	?	?	?	?	*
IN	IN	accumulator,port	—	—	—	—	—	—	—	—	—
INC	INC	destination	*	—	—	—	*	*	*	*	—
INT	INT	interrupt-type	—	—	0	0	—	—	—	—	—
INTO	INTO		—	—	0	0	—	—	—	—	—
IRET	IRET		*	*	*	*	*	*	*	*	*
JA/JNBE	JA	short-label	—	—	—	—	—	—	—	—	—
JAE/JNB	JAE	short-label	—	—	—	—	—	—	—	—	—
JB/JNAE/JC	JB	short-label	—	—	—	—	—	—	—	—	—
JBE/JNA	JBE	short-label	—	—	—	—	—	—	—	—	—
JCXZ	JCXZ	short-label	—	—	—	—	—	—	—	—	—
JE/JZ	JE	short-label	—	—	—	—	—	—	—	—	—
JC/JNLE	JG	short-label	—	—	—	—	—	—	—	—	—
JGE/JNL	JGE	short-label	—	—	—	—	—	—	—	—	—
JL/JNGE	JL	short-label	—	—	—	—	—	—	—	—	—
JLE/JNG	JLE	short-label	—	—	—	—	—	—	—	—	—
JMP	JMP	target	—	—	—	—	—	—	—	—	—
JNC	JNC	short-label	—	—	—	—	—	—	—	—	—
JNE/JNZ	JNE	short-label	—	—	—	—	—	—	—	—	—
JNO	JNO	short-label	—	—	—	—	—	—	—	—	—
JNP/JPO	JNP	short-label	—	—	—	—	—	—	—	—	—
JNS	JNS	short-label	—	—	—	—	—	—	—	—	—
JO	JO	short-label	—	—	—	—	—	—	—	—	—
JP/JPE	JP	short-label	—	—	—	—	—	—	—	—	—
JS	JS	short-label	—	—	—	—	—	—	—	—	—
LAHF	LAHF		—	—	—	—	—	—	—	—	—
LDS	LDS	reg16,mem32	—	—	—	—	—	—	—	—	—
LEA	LEA	reg16,mem16	—	—	—	—	—	—	—	—	—
LES	LES	reg16,mem32	—	—	—	—	—	—	—	—	—
LOCK	LOCK		—	—	—	—	—	—	—	—	—
LODS	LODS	source-string	—	—	—	—	—	—	—	—	—
LODSB	LODSB		—	—	—	—	—	—	—	—	—
LODSW	LODSW		—	—	—	—	—	—	—	—	—
LOOP	LOOP	short-label	—	—	—	—	—	—	—	—	—

Table D–1. 8086/8088 instruction set (continued).

Mnemonic	Assembler Format		OF	DF	IF	TF	SF	ZF	AF	PF	CF
						Flags					
LOOPE/ LOOPZ	LOOPE	short-label	—	—	—	—	—	—	—	—	—
LOOPNE/ LOOPNZ	LOOPNE	short-label	—	—	—	—	—	—	—	—	—
MOV	MOV	destination,source	—	—	—	—	—	—	—	—	—
MOVS	MOVS	dest-string,source-string	—	—	—	—	—	—	—	—	—
MOVSB	MOVSB		—	—	—	—	—	—	—	—	—
MOVSW	MOVSW		—	—	—	—	—	—	—	—	—
MUL	MUL	source	*	—	—	—	?	?	?	?	*
NEG	NEG	destination	*	—	—	—	*	*	*	*	*
NOP	NOP		—	—	—	—	—	—	—	—	—
NOT	NOT	destination	—	—	—	—	—	—	—	—	—
OR	OR	destination,source	0	—	—	—	*	*	?	*	0
OUT	OUT	port,accumulator	—	—	—	—	—	—	—	—	—
POP	POP	destination	—	—	—	—	—	—	—	—	—
POPF	POPF		*	*	*	*	*	*	*	*	*
PUSH	PUSH	source	—	—	—	—	—	—	—	—	—
PUSHF	PUSHF		—	—	—	—	—	—	—	—	—
RCL	RCL	destination,count	*	—	—	—	—	—	—	—	*
RCR	RCR	destination,count	*	—	—	—	—	—	—	—	*
REP	REP		—	—	—	—	—	—	—	—	—
REPE/REPZ	REPE		—	—	—	—	—	—	—	—	—
REPNE/ REPNZ	REPNE		—	—	—	—	—	—	—	—	—
RET	[pop-value]		—	—	—	—	—	—	—	—	—
ROL	ROL	destination,count	*	—	—	—	—	—	—	—	*
ROR	ROR	destination,count	*	—	—	—	—	—	—	—	*
SAHF	SAHF		—	—	—	—	*	*	*	*	*
SAL/SHL	SAL	destination,count	*	—	—	—	*	*	?	*	*
SAR	SAR	destination,count	*	—	—	—	*	*	?	*	*
SBB	SBB	destination,source	*	—	—	—	*	*	*	*	*
SCAS	SCAS	dest-string	*	—	—	—	*	*	*	*	*
SCASB	SCASB		*	—	—	—	*	*	*	*	*
SCASW	SCASW		*	—	—	—	*	*	*	*	*
SHR	SHR	destination,count	*	—	—	—	0	*	?	*	*
STC	STC		—	—	—	—	—	—	—	—	1
STD	STD		—	1	—	—	—	—	—	—	—
STI	STI		—	—	1	—	—	—	—	—	—
STOS	STOS	dest-string	—	—	—	—	—	—	—	—	—
STOSB	STOSB		—	—	—	—	—	—	—	—	—
STOSW	STOSW		—	—	—	—	—	—	—	—	—
SUB	SUB	destination,source	*	—	—	—	*	*	*	*	*

Table D–1. 8086/8088 instruction set (continued).

Mnemonic	Assembler Format		OF	DF	IF	TF	SF	ZF	AF	PF	CF
					Flags						
TEST	TEST	destination,source	0	—	—	—	*	*	?	*	0
WAIT	WAIT		—	—	—	—	—	—	—	—	—
XCHG	XCHG	destination,source	—	—	—	—	—	—	—	—	—
XLAT	XLAT	source-table	—	—	—	—	—	—	—	—	—
XOR	XOR	destination,source	0	—	—	—	*	*	?	*	0

Answers to Study Exercises

Chapter 0. A Crash Course in Computer Numbering Systems (page 7)
1. (a) 1100   (b) 10001   (c) 101101   (d) 1001000
2. (a) 8   (b) 21   (c) 31
3. (a) 8   (b) 15   (c) 1F
4. The hexadecimal value D8 can represent the unsigned number 216 or the signed number −40. The signed number is derived by converting the hexadecimal value to binary (11011000), then reversing each bit (which gives 00100111) and adding 1 (which gives 00101000, or decimal 40).

Chapter 1. Introduction to Assembly Language Programming (page 22)
1. There is *no* difference between the instruction set of the 8088 and that of the 8086—they are identical.
2. When calculating a physical address, the 8086 automatically appends four zeros to the segment number to form the segment *address*. Therefore, it uses 4000H as 40000H and calculates the physical address as

```
Physical address = 2H + 40000H = 40002H
```

3. If the AX register contains 1A2BH, AL (the low-order byte of AX) contains 2BH.
4. Variables are usually stored in the data segment, so the Data Segment (DS) register is normally used to access them.
5. Bit 7, the Sign Flag (SF), is set to 1 if a subtraction gives a negative result.

Chapter 2. Using an Assembler (page 50)
1. The assembler allocates 1 byte for VAR1, 10 bytes (five words = 10 bytes) for VAR2, and 10 bytes for VAR3, for a total of *21* bytes.
2. The assembler doesn't put any value into VAR1. The ? operand tells the assembler simply to *reserve* 1 byte for VAR1. Your program must put something into VAR1.

   Note that the assembler puts a value into only one location here: it puts 20 into the fifth word of VAR2. All other locations are "undefined."
3. CONST is a *byte* variable, and cannot hold values greater than 255.
4. Every procedure starts with PROC and ends with ENDP.
5. You can call a NEAR procedure only from within the segment in which

it is defined. You can call a FAR procedure from any segment in the program.

6. The END pseudo-op must appear at the end of every source program, so that the assembler knows when to stop assembling.

Chapter 3. The 8086 Instruction Set (page 119)

1. The instruction is MOV ES:SAVE__AX,AX.
2. The sequence shown stores 0 into the first location of the data segment (addressed by BX) and the stack segment (addressed by BP).
3. a. *Invalid*. A constant cannot be a destination.
   b. *Valid*, but since TEMP has not been initialized, you will get "garbage" in AL.
   c. *Invalid*. You can't move a word value into a byte variable.
   d. *Invalid*. The MOV instruction cannot be used to make a direct memory-to-memory transfer.
   e. *Invalid*. The assembler does not recognize the addressing form [BX][BP]. See Table 3–1 for valid operand formats.
4. These instructions clear the AX register:

```
SUB AX,AX
MOV AX,0
```

5. These instructions are identical. Both load the offset of location TABLE + 4 into BX. LEA, however, is both shorter and more explicit.
6. This loop subtracts V2 from V1:

```
        MOV     CX,3            ;Word count = 3
        MOV     BX,0            ;Offset = 0
        CLC                     ;Clear Carry (CF)
NEXT:   MOV     DX,V2[BX]       ;Subtract words
        SBB     V1[BX],DX
        INC     BX              ; and address next
                                ; word
        INC     BX
        LOOP    NEXT
```

Note that BX is increased by 2 after each subtraction because words lie 2 bytes apart in memory. We use two INCs rather than one ADD so as not to affect the Carry Flag (CF), which is included in the SBB operation.

7. This MUL instruction generates an error. You cannot multiply by an immediate value.
8. The results are as follows:
   a. (AX) = 0220H
   b. (AX) = 5335H
   c. (AX) = 5115H
   d. (AX) = 0EDCBH
   e. (AX) = 1234H (Because TEST affects only the flags)

9. The sequence to normalize AX is:

```
              TEST    AX,0FFFFH
              JZ      NORM        ;Exit if (AX) = 0
              MOV     CX,15       ;Get set for 15
                                  ; shifts
NEXT_BIT:     JS      NORM        ;Exit if Bit 15 =
                                  ; 1
              SHL     AX,1        ;Otherwise, shift
                                  ; AX left by one
              LOOP    NEXT_BIT
NORM:         ..
              ..
```

10. If you said the sequence subtracts 30 from AX, look again. LOOP decrements CX, then jumps to START if CX is zero. The MOV instruction,
however, continually reinitializes CX to 3, so CX will *never* reach zero.
This kind of endless loop is a common programming error. Watch out
for it.

Chapter 4. High-Precision Mathematics (page 135)

1. This procedure extracts a square root by subtracting successively higher
odd numbers:

```
SR32      PROC
          PUSH    AX        ;Save original number
          PUSH    DX
          PUSH    CX        ; and CX on the stack
          MOV     BX,1      ;To start, (BX) = 1
          SUB     CX,CX     ; and (CX) = 0
AGAIN:    SUB     AX,BX     ;Subtract next odd
                            ; number from AX
          SBB     DX,0      ; and DX
          JC      DONE      ;Did this subtraction
                            ; create a borrow?
          INC     CX        ; No. Increase the
                            ; square root by 1,
          ADD     BX,2      ; calculate the next odd
                            ; number,
          JMP     AGAIN     ; then make the next
                            ; subtraction
DONE:     MOV     BX,CX     ; Yes. Transfer result
                            ; to BX
          POP     CX        ; and restore the
                            ; registers
          POP     DX
          POP     AX
          RET
SR32      ENDP
```

Chapter 5. Operating on Data Structures (page 170)

1. This modified version of Example 5–1 can be used to build a list from scratch, as well as add a new element to an existing list:

```
ADD_TO_UL  PROC
           PUSH    DI              ;Save starting
                                   ; address
           MOV     CX,ES:[DI]      ;Fetch word
                                   ; count
           ADD     DI,2            ;Make DI point
                                   ; to first
                                   ; element
           CMP     CX,0            ;Is the list
                                   ; null?
           JE      ADD_IT          ; Yes. Value
                                   ; is first
                                   ; element
           CLD                     ; No. Set DF =
                                   ;  0
  REPNE    SCASW                   ;Value already
                                   ; in the list?
           JNE     ADD_IT
           POP     DI              ; Yes. Restore
                                   ; starting
                                   ; address
           RET                     ; and exit
ADD_IT:    STOSW                   ; No. Add it
                                   ; to end of
                                   ; list
           POP     DI              ; then update
                                   ; element
                                   ; count
           INC     WORD PTR ES:[DI]
           RET
ADD_TO_UL  ENDP
```

2. Here is the find-and-replace procedure:

```
; This procedure searches an ordered list in
; the extra segment to the word value
; contained in AX. If a matching element is
; found, its contents are replaced with the
; value in BX.
; AX and BX are unaffected.
;
REPLACE    PROC
           CALL    B_SEARCH        ;Is the search
                                   ; value in the
                                   ; list?
```

```
            JC     QUIT          ; If not, exit
            MOV    ES:[SI],BX    ; Is so, replace
                                 ; it with BX
QUIT:       RET
REPLACE     ENDP
```

Index